Bosses, Coworkers, and Building Great Work Relationships

D1636669

HBR Work Smart Series

*Rise faster with quick reads,
real stories, and expert advice.*

It's not easy to navigate the world of work when you're exploring who you are and what you want in life. How do you translate your interests, skills, and education into building a career you love?

The **HBR Work Smart Series** features the topics that matter to you most in your early career, including being yourself at work, collaborating with (sometimes difficult) colleagues and bosses, managing your mental health, and weighing major job decisions. Each title includes chapter recaps and links to video, audio, and more. The HBR Work Smart books are your practical guides to stepping into your professional life and moving forward with confidence.

Books in the series include:

Authenticity, Identity, and Being Yourself at Work

Bosses, Coworkers, and Building Great Work Relationships

Boundaries, Priorities, and Finding Work-Life Balance

Experience, Opportunity, and Developing Your Career

WORK
SMART

*Tips for Navigating
Your Career*

Bosses, Coworkers, and **Building Great Work Relationships**

**HARVARD BUSINESS
REVIEW PRESS**
Boston, Massachusetts

Library of Congress Cataloging-in-Publication Data

Names: Harvard Business Review Press, issuing body.
Title: Bosses, coworkers, and building great work relationships / Harvard Business Review.
Description: Boston, Massachusetts: Harvard Business Review Press, [2024] | Series: HBR work smart series | Includes index. |
Identifiers: LCCN 2023048536 (print) | LCCN 2023048537 (ebook) | ISBN 9781647827113 (paperback) | ISBN 9781647827120 (epub)
Subjects: LCSH: Quality of work life. | Interpersonal relations. | Emotional intelligence. | Psychology, Industrial.
Classification: LCC HD4904 .B657 2024 (print) | LCC HD4904 (ebook) | DDC 331.01—dc23/eng/20231201
LC record available at https://lccn.loc.gov/2023048536
LC ebook record available at https://lccn.loc.gov/2023048537

ISBN: 978-1-64782-711-3
eISBN: 978-1-64782-712-0

CONTENTS

SECTION 1
Bosses, Managers, and Higher-Ups

SECTION 2

Coworkers, Teammates, and Work Friends

SECTION 3

Networks, Mentors, and Sponsors

The Two Key Ingredients to Great Work Relationships

by Eliana Goldstein

I opened the email from my coaching client Sara and could immediately sense her panic. "Eliana! Can we schedule an emergency coaching session?! I just received a request from my manager asking if we could get a one-on-one meeting on the calendar. We just had one last week, so I have no idea what this is about. My mind is racing!" Sara was an ambitious project manager who had been working at her company for over two years. She was on good terms with her manager, usually excelled in her role, and her company seemed secure and stable. My gut told me her boss's request was nothing to be concerned about. Even so, I wanted to speak with Sara, both to reassure her in the moment and to explore why this message triggered such a stress response. What else was going on, and how might this kind of thinking be holding her back elsewhere at work?

As we chatted, Sara shared her fears and thought processes. She was concerned that she wasn't being proactive enough in how she approached her job and that her manager thus perceived her as unmotivated. This stream of worries ended with her being fired. I did my best to reassure Sara that based on her track record, I was confident this one-on-one was not what she imagined. We moved on to discussing how she could harness her fear. If a one-on-one request was making her so anxious, she needed to create more stability in her work life. She agreed and reflected that at her core, she wanted to be more strategic in how she handled her career going forward, but didn't know where to start.

Fast-forward a few days. Sara had her one-on-one, and instead of all the catastrophes she had imagined, it was a very positive discussion. Her manager was pleased with Sara's work on a recent project and wanted to get her thoughts on a new internal team the company was developing. Sara was even invited to help build out that team!

So the question you may be asking yourself is, *Why?* Why did Sara, a well-respected go-getter and a hardworking employee, spiral into a complete state of panic when she received a simple request for a meeting with her manager? She's not alone. The truth is that for many young professionals, navigating office relationships can feel overwhelming and intimidating.

I hear a lot of these stories from my millennial and Gen Z coaching clients. Perhaps like many, you worked hard in school, figured out how to stand out among a sea of applicants, and earned the prized golden ticket: You got a great job! But a lot of high achievers make a mistake early in their careers: They put such an emphasis on getting the job that once they have it, they charge ahead and dive straight into the work. They focus on deadlines and deliverables instead of connecting and collaborating. Then, six months or a year later, they find themselves in Sara's position. They've delivered good results, but they feel anxious and out of the loop because they haven't built quality relationships with their managers and peers.

Here's what I tell all my clients: Strong work relationships are the secret sauce for reducing stress, expediting your growth, and even managing your career. You may have noticed that the people who tend to grow quickly, get the promotions, and get the raises aren't always the ones who are the best at their jobs. But you know what they are probably *really* good at? Building work relationships. It's surprisingly simple, and there are just two key ingredients:

- Building strong connections with the right people

- Being purposeful in your conversations and asking the right questions

Just two ingredients, but they entail *a lot*. Fortunately, they're exactly what this book will be diving into in detail.

Let's start with the first. In section 1, you will learn more about how to build stronger connections with the higher-ups at your organization. This doesn't simply mean getting to know your manager, their likes and dislikes, how many kids they have, or what they do for fun. Sure, that's important too, but it's *really* about creating internal visibility and a value exchange with them. You want to build a relationship that allows you to contribute to your company while doing your job better, learning how to think more expansively about your role, and preparing for your next steps. You'll learn how to take the lead in these conversations in coach and consultant Antoinette Oglethorpe's "How to Talk to Your Boss About Your Career Development."

Another essential part of relationship building at work? Quality connections with the people who are in the thick of it with you. Section 2 covers how to develop relationships with your coworkers. Whether work is going great or not so great, having a mutual support system to lean on is vital. You'll learn about topics like how to build trust when you are new to a team and how to make work friends across age differences. Another reality at work is that you're going to have some difficult coworkers. Perhaps they take credit for your work, or they speak to you in a way that you don't appreciate. HBR editor Vasundhara Sawhney will walk you through such situations in "How to Give Negative Feedback to Your Peer."

Building relationships with higher-ups and your coworkers can happen in the flow of your day. But there's another group—who may just be the most influential in your career—and you'll probably need to seek them out: They are your network, mentors, and sponsors. Regardless of where you are in your career—employed or unemployed, junior or senior, well-connected or not—developing your network and finding mentors is something that you should consistently be doing. Don't think you can wait until later in your career. Holly Raider's "How to Strengthen Your Network When You're Just Starting Out" offers guidance here, and Janice Omadeke will help you understand the difference between a mentor and a sponsor and why you need both of them.

You won't be getting much out of these relationships—and really, you won't have much success building them—if you're talking about the wrong things. So let's move onto the second key ingredient: approaching your conversations with purpose and asking the right questions. Purposeful conversations at work can be tough and uncomfortable. It's a lot easier to talk about your commute, your lunch, or how busy you are. Fortunately, this book has dozens of ideas to get you started, from what questions to ask your boss in one-on-ones to how to have graceful talks about politics at work. The more you engage in difficult conversations and the more questions you ask to better understand how your role fits into the bigger picture, the easier these conversations become. Before you know it, you'll feel your confidence growing, and you'll know you're on the track to being a relationship-building, career-growing, success-destined machine!

Think of this book as the Career Navigation 101 crash course that you never took before joining the workforce. While right now conversations with your manager may feel intimidating, and it can seem impossible to find a mentor, remind yourself that anything new often does feel challenging. Don't worry: Relationship building in the working world *is* a distinct challenge to almost everyone who is just starting out in a professional setting. This is because the mental muscles you use to build relationships at work are *not* identical to the ones you use outside of work. Accept that now and you can begin building skills that will help you succeed today and throughout your career.

This brings us back to Sara. In our next meeting, we talked about the two key ingredients, and she committed to trying them out. She started by flipping the script and *asked* her manager for a one-on-one. Prior to chatting, she sketched out a career map for herself, one that identified short- and long-term goals she wanted to work toward, relationships she would need to build across the organization to facilitate those goals, and ways she believed she could add value to her direct team and organization going forward. Then she shared her plan, listened to her boss's thoughts and feedback, and brainstormed together with her boss on next steps she could take. With her biggest fear at work managed, Sarah is happier and dedicating more time to doing her job better. Whatever your biggest relationship challenge at work, I hope the advice, strategies, and stories in this book can help you conquer it and put you on the right path forward.

Bosses, Managers, and Higher-Ups

How to Talk to Your Boss About Your Career Development

by Antoinette Oglethorpe

Some people enter the workforce thinking their manager is responsible for their career development. They work hard, deliver results, and wait to be promoted.

Unfortunately, this strategy rarely works.

What no one has told them is: Your career development starts with you—and is amplified by the support of your manager. To advance in any role, you need to proactively initiate a career-planning conversation with your boss. This is a meeting you can use to discuss your interest in growth opportunities, ensure that your individual goals are aligned with the mission of the organization, and develop a longer-term plan to set you up for success.

If this sounds like a lot of work to you, you're correct. Career conversations take significant planning and preparation, but in the end, you will walk away with a better idea of how to advance. Here is a step-by-step guide to help you get proactive about your growth and set up a productive career conversation with your boss.

Ahead of the Meeting

Start by reflecting on what you want

Before approaching your boss, you need to have a clear under-standing of where you are right now and where you want to be in a few years. This will help you verbalize your professional goals and create a development plan in service of them. Set aside some time in your schedule to reflect on your status and your future goals. Ask yourself the following questions:

Where are you now? Think about the tasks you do on a daily basis as well as any projects or priorities on your plate. Which aspects of this work do you find energizing versus draining? Which areas do you consistently feel confident in and which do you consistently struggle with?

Take stock of whether you have mastered the skills needed to succeed at your current level. Gaining this clarity will allow you to more intentionally seek out opportunities where you can lever-age your strengths and also identify stretch projects you can use for growth and improvement.

Also seek feedback from peers. Does your analysis of your strengths and weaknesses match theirs? What, in their eyes, sets you apart from others?

What's important to you in the long term? The goal of this question is to help you identify your values and how they fit into your work. You need to understand this to create a development plan that will help you build a fulfilling career.

Think about what you want to do next. What kind of role do you see yourself in two years from now? When you imagine this dream job, what are you willing to compromise on and what is nonnegotiable?

Recall the tasks that you found most energizing. For example, you might realize that administrative tasks drain you and interacting with clients energizes you. How does this fit into your image of the future? How does it fit into your next role at your current organization? Perhaps being promoted into a role that includes more face time with clients is a nonnegotiable, whereas administrative work is something you will need to negotiate or compromise on. This information will be valuable during your career conversation with your boss.

Before moving on, as a last consideration, think about how your ambitions align with the mission or goals of your team and organization. If you can connect your future goals back to the goals of the company, you can present your manager with a more convincing argument for your growth.

What does success look like to you? Success means different things to different people—an upward trajectory is just one version. Maybe, upon reflection, you've realized that you don't want to take on more responsibility or become a people manager. Maybe, to you, success involves more work-life balance and heads-down creative work. Define your version of success so that your manager understands your ambitions and can help you reach them.

Request a meeting with your manager

A career conversation should not be folded into your weekly one-on-one or tagged onto your performance review. It should be a separate meeting specifically focused on discussing career growth. The frequency of these conversations will vary, but ideally your manager should be open to holding them several times a year to allow for ongoing feedback, goal setting and alignment, and discussion of new or upcoming career development opportunities. It's usually best to have them shortly after an annual or semiannual performance review—when you've already spent time reflecting on your past work—and can now develop a forward-looking plan.

When requesting a career conversation, be clear about the purpose of the meeting. Email your manager and suggest meeting at their convenience within the next week, giving them time to prepare.

During the Meeting

Start on a positive note

Begin the conversation by expressing gratitude for the opportunity. You could say, "Thank you so much for meeting with me today—I really appreciate it. I'd like to use this time to discuss my career aspirations and, hopefully, come up with a development plan that will help me align my goals with our larger team goals and the goals of the company."

Next, clearly articulate your insights from your self-reflection time. Explain where you see yourself currently, including the aspects of your role that you find fulfilling and those you would like to grow in, change, or develop in new ways. For instance, you might say, "I feel most fulfilled when I'm working with clients and think that my welcoming and clear communication style is a strength that sets me apart on the team."

Move on to recapping your achievements and highlight how they have contributed to the success of your team or company. This will not only demonstrate your value but also provide a foundation for the conversation around your growth. You could say: "Over the past year, I successfully led the X project, which resulted in a Y% increase in client engagement—contributing to the organizational goal of increasing client engagement by Z%. I believe this shows my potential to take on more challenging client-facing roles on our team and coach others on how to successfully do the same."

Follow up by sharing what's important to you in the next stage of your career and how you see those changes contributing to your long-term growth: "As I grow at the company, I'd love to continue taking on more client-facing projects and eventually leading them. I see this as a way to further develop my communication skills and evolve as a people leader, which is a role I want to grow into."

Finally, if there are development areas you want to acknowledge, don't ignore them. Instead, connect them back to the vision of the organization. You could add, "I know I still have more to learn about project management, and taking on more initiatives will allow me to do this. The company wants to increase our client outreach this year, so my growth would help contribute to that goal." Remember, your career goals should create a win-win situation for both you and the organization.

Identify next steps

You've just given your manager a lot to think about, and it may take them some time to consider before responding. After making your case, follow up with something like, "I'm curious to hear your thoughts and feedback."

In some cases, your manager may thank you for opening up the discussion and ask to revisit the conversation in a week—giving them more time to process and come up with a plan. In the best-case scenario, your manager will have come more prepared, with their own ideas about where they can see you growing. In this case, you can work together to develop next steps.

Start by discussing the following areas:

- *Understanding the opportunities available to you.* Ask your manager what opportunities are available to you given your goals and aspirations. Do you need to learn new skills before moving up the ladder? If so, what are they and how can you better demonstrate them? Do they feel you are ready to take on a stretch project? If there are no opportunities on your team, is there another team you could work with in order to grow?

- *Navigating the processes and politics of the organization.* Your manager is not the sole decision-maker in most cases, especially when it comes to promotions. You need to understand how the organization works, including both processes and tactics; who the key influencers are; and how to raise your profile and be more visible to key people. Ask your boss, "Are there other people in the organization whose work I should be observing more closely? I would love to speak with them and learn how they've become successful here. How would you suggest I make my work and myself more visible?"

- *Identifying and evaluating different options and opportunities.* It's unlikely that you and your manager will put together an elaborate plan in this first meeting. Once your manager presents you with options, thank them for their insights. Then let them know that you will think about what you discussed. Ask if you can take some time to outline a more tangible plan for them to review in a follow-up meeting. This will give you the space you need to reflect on the pros and cons of your discussion and propose a few solid next steps.

After the Meeting

Draft a development plan

Take what you've learned and put together a plan that outlines next steps, including any new skills you need to acquire, any projects you've agreed to take on, and any important stakeholders you want to begin building relationships with.

Remember, the best plans are both ambitious and realistic, pushing your boundaries while still being achievable. Use SMART (specific, measurable, achievable, relevant, time-bound) goals so you can monitor your progress over time. While there will always be factors that are out of your control, it's useful to structure your plan using concrete milestones (even if they are subject to change). For instance, setting a goal like "finishing the leadership training program within six months" or "increasing client engagement by 10% in Q2" are more feasible than something unpredictable like "be promoted to people leader by fall of 2024."

Follow up

Once you've outlined your goals and milestones, set up some time to review your plan with your manager. Try to do this no later than a week after that first meeting so that the conversation is still top of mind. It can be helpful to send your manager your plan prior to your discussion to give them time to review it thoughtfully beforehand.

Use your follow-up meeting to gather their feedback, make adjustments, and ensure that you're both aligned. Then ask if you can check in on how things are progressing—either in additional follow-up meetings or during your regular check-ins throughout the year.

.   .   .

Career conversations are vital to your professional growth. By initiating them, you make your ambitions known, gain valuable feedback, and pave the way for a fulfilling career path. Prepare well, communicate clearly, and always be open to feedback. In doing so, you'll empower yourself to move forward, secure the knowledge you need to grow, and give your manager an opportunity to fully understand and support you on your journey.

QUICK RECAP

To advance in any role, you should proactively initiate a career-planning conversation with your boss. In this meeting, you can show your interest in growth opportunities, ensure that your goals are aligned with the organization's, and develop a plan to set you up for success.

- Start with self-reflection to better understand where you are now and where you want to be in a few years.

- Request a meeting with your manager to specifically discuss your career growth.

- During the meeting, share your insights from your self-reflection. Highlight how your achievements have contributed to the success of your team or company.

- After the meeting, draft a forward-looking plan that outlines next steps, and follow up with your manager.

Adapted from content posted on hbr.org, August 1, 2023.

2

Twenty-Eight Questions to Ask Your Manager in Your One-on-Ones

by Steven G. Rogelberg, Liana Kreamer, and Cydnei Meredith

When she started a new role, Brianna was told she would be having regular one-on-one meetings (1:1s) with her manager, Jayden. She welcomed this news; she saw it as a great opportunity to get aligned with and supported and mentored by her new boss. But her hopes were quickly dashed. In their initial meeting, Jayden focused only on project updates and then assigned her a few additional tasks. This pattern continued over the weeks, and Brianna routinely left their meetings feeling both micromanaged and unsupported in her development.

This story is, sadly, a composite of many we have heard from employees in our research on 1:1s between managers and their direct reports. Good one-on-one meetings address both the practical (information, instruction, alignment) and personal (consideration, respect, trust, and support) needs of the employee. These meetings are a critical source of growth and support for the employee and promote the thriving and success of teams and the broader organization.

But these benefits are only realized when the meeting includes frequent conversations that address those employee needs. And as 1:1s are typically facilitated by managers, they often devolve into addressing what is front of mind for them, rather than the employee. That's especially true because managers rarely receive training on how to run these meetings well, so they often recycle dysfunctional practices they themselves have experienced.

If you are in Brianna's position—if your boss's approach to your 1:1s has left you feeling unsupported and unheard—you should feel empowered to direct the conversation toward your needs yourself. You can do this by asking smart questions.

Questions to Ask

Based on published research as well as data we collected from nearly 200 employees on important topics to broach in a 1:1, we have identified 28 key questions in seven broad categories to help you get the most value from your check-ins with your boss. You can use, adapt, and put these into your own voice as you see fit.

Ask for guidance and input

Use these questions to get help from your manager on any tasks or projects you are having difficulty with or to express your need for additional resources, input, or support.

1. I am having some challenges and struggles with X. Can you help me think about how to navigate and address X successfully?

2. Could you suggest any ideas and thoughts around how I could get more support (people, time, funding) to help with Y?

3. What do you think of my idea Z? Do you have any suggestions for how to improve it? Or might you have an alternative idea I should consider?

Clarify priorities and expectations

To be sure you are on track and working efficiently, make sure you and your manager are on the same page. Ask for clarification on what tasks need your most focused attention.

4. Given what's on my plate, what should I be prioritizing right now, and can you help me understand why?

5. As you review my workload, am I taking on the right projects and tasks?

6. Am I on track for meeting my goals and your expectations from your perspective? Is any refocusing necessary?

7. Is there any context I might be missing about the projects I am working on? For example, what is the reasoning for doing project X?

Align with the organization and its strategy

Ask questions to understand how your role relates to the broader strategic goals of the organization and the way its leaders are thinking about the future.

8. What is going on further up the tree (or in other parts of the organization) that would be helpful for me to know as I work on my key tasks?

9. To better help me understand the big picture, how does the work I'm doing or the assignment you just gave me fit into the broader goals and strategy?

10. Is there anything that the management team is working on or considering that you think I should know about, given its potential impact on my role?

11. What is new in our strategic priorities as a company that you feel I should know about, if anything?

Seek growth opportunities and career advancement

Come to the meeting with your thoughts (however inchoate) around your professional short-term and long-term goals and ask your manager what steps you should take to get there.

12. I would value your counsel. What can I do to prepare myself for greater opportunities or to pursue X interest of mine?

13. As you reflect on where the organization is going, do you have any thoughts on how I should improve and develop to best align?

14. What strengths do you think I have, and how might they be helpful in the future?

15. From your perspective, what should I be targeting as my next career move, and why do you recommend that position?

16. How can we make sure that my skill set is put to the best use to support the team and the organization?

17. How can we make sure that my full potential is achieved?

Get feedback on your performance

Check in with your manager to see how you are doing. You shouldn't make every meeting into an official performance evaluation, but it is important to periodically check in and calibrate if your manager isn't doing that themselves.

18. Am I meeting your expectations? I would really like to hear your perspective on my work performance.

19. What feedback might you be able to share with me about how I'm doing at X or Y task?

20. Do you feel there are any spots I'm overlooking when it comes to A or B?

21. As you reflect on what I do at work, what should I start, stop, or continue doing?

Build a relationship

Your 1:1 is a critical place for you to build and nurture your relationship with your manager. Allocate time at the beginning or end of the meeting to connect with them personally.

22. How is your day going?

23. How are things going for you overall? Are you doing OK?

24. What is something you are excited about outside of work?

25. Is there anything you would like to know about me? (If needed, be prepared to say, "I don't feel comfortable sharing that, but here's something else you should know about me.")

Offer support

Consider ways in which you can help your manager achieve their goals and fulfill their role. Managers need assistance, reassurance, and support to optimize their efficiency and performance. Just like you'd expect your manager to support you, see how you can lend them a hand. This will also increase the chances of you getting what you need in the 1:1.

26. What are your priorities over the next X days? What can I do to help you with this?

27. Where can I offer you support?

28. Is there anything keeping you up at night that I can help with?

How to Use the Questions

For each 1:1 meeting, pick a category or two to focus on. You can't address them all in every meeting, so you will need to rotate or pick the most relevant at a given time. Likewise, choose sparingly from among the questions—no need to ask them all at one time. You'll simply want to sample from all categories over time.

Don't hesitate to follow up on your manager's responses to your questions. A great follow-up is often simply "Why?" You'll glean strategic insights into the rationale, motives, assumptions, and big picture behind your day-to-day work.

Good 1:1 meetings with your manager are critical for your success and the success of your team and organization. Asking the right questions to make sure those meetings give you what you need can have a huge impact on your work experience—helping you stay engaged, developing your understanding of your role and place in the organization, and improving your relationship with your manager—not to mention enhancing your well-being.

QUICK RECAP

Good 1:1 meetings with your manager address your practical and personal needs, benefiting your performance, growth, and well-being as well as the success of your team and the broader organization. Twenty-eight questions can drive the best conversations in your 1:1s. These questions fall into seven broad categories:

- Asking for guidance and input

- Clarifying priorities and expectations

- Aligning with the organization and its strategy

- Seeking growth opportunities and career advancement

- Getting feedback on your performance

- Building a relationship

- Offering support

Adapted from "28 Questions to Ask Your Boss in Your One-on-Ones" on hbr.org, June 23, 2023.

Three Ways to Say No to Your Boss

by Paige Cohen

How often have you heard the job advice: "Say yes to everything"? The idea is that the more work you take on, the greater ambition you'll show and the faster you'll move ahead in the organization. This wisdom was passed down to me through many generations—mentors, teachers, bosses, senior colleagues, and parents. Early in my career, I made them proud. I rarely, if ever, turned down a task.

I had an endless to-do list and spent late hours at the office paying my dues. Who cared if I was completely burned out and had no idea what I enjoyed or wanted to do? I was blessed with endless "opportunities." I was showing off great skills, like organization and efficiency. I was a yes person—the best kind of person. What could be better than that?

Years later, I have the answer to that question: learning when to say no. It took me a lot of trial and error to come to this, but gracefully turning people down has gotten me much farther than taking on nonpromotable tasks for fear of disappointing others. Strategically saying no can afford you more energy, time, and work-life balance. It's a talent: the ability to prioritize work that will showcase your strengths or focus on tasks that will help you develop the skills you need to advance to the next level.

Like me, early in your career, you may feel more pressure to say yes to everything. It makes sense. You're new. You're trying to build a good reputation. But remember: Reserving your energy for the most important work—the work that will benefit you and your ambitions—will make you more successful than taking on tasks you don't have the bandwidth to handle.

Still, saying no is hard to do, especially if the request comes from your boss. So how do you do it?

I asked my team members, each of whom have a great deal of experience in this area, for advice.

How to Say No to Your Boss

Take a day to think about whether the task will help or hurt you

Saying no to my boss (or even my coworkers) is something I've always struggled with. I began my career in the startup world. As a member of a very small team, I learned the value of saying yes to every task thrown my way—even those that were far outside my job description. Not only did I learn a lot by doing so, but I also gained my boss's favor and earned promotions quickly as a result. I still carry this mentality with me even though I work at a much bigger company now.

I still think saying yes to tasks outside of your comfort zone can be really rewarding, but I also now understand the challenges that can come with doing so. If you say yes to everything, you're basically saying no to doing a good job at anything. There's a point at which spreading yourself too thin will cause a dip in your performance, and all of that goodwill and experience you would have gained by trying something new goes out the window.

Now, when my boss asks me if I can take on a new task or project, I try to create a pause in the conversation by saying something like, "That sounds interesting! Would you mind if I get back to you tomorrow so I can look at my other priorities right now and see how much time I'd have to help out?"

From there, I try to think about the task itself and ask myself a few questions:

- Will I learn something new or gain experience by saying yes?

- Does this task align with my future career goals?

- What experiences will I lose out on if I say yes to this task?

- Am I already feeling overwhelmed?

These questions help me sort out if I'm actually interested in helping out with the project at hand, or if I'm just saying yes because I want to make my boss happy.

-Kelsey Alpaio (she/her),
Senior Associate Editor, HBR Ascend

Don't just say no; explain why you're saying it

There's an uneven power dynamic when someone more senior than you asks you to take on a task. That's why it's important to outline the logic behind your answer, especially if you turn them down. Simply saying no leaves room for the requester to assume why you won't accept a task or are declining a project. Context is vital.

Examples of reasons you might say no include:

- You can't finish the task or project within the required time frame.

- You don't feel you have the resources to do the work successfully.

- You'll have to neglect important responsibilities to get the new task done.

In other words, if saying no will lead to a more efficient, balanced, and successful version of both you and your work, it's probably the right answer. As with most conversations at work, it's best to be transparent about what you notice, feel, and believe.

I suggest using phrases like, "I wouldn't feel comfortable doing this because . . ." or "With my current workload, I won't be able to finish this task within the time you'll need." Sharing your logic with your boss will help frame you as a thoughtful, responsible, honest, and reasonable colleague.

–Nicole D. Smith (she/her),
Editorial Audience Director, HBR

Support your reasoning with data

Overloading yourself with tasks that you can't perform at your best will only lead to subpar results. When you say no to your boss, it's your job to make them understand that by using data and evidence to support your case.

The first step is to clearly understand the requirements of the task and estimate the efforts needed to complete it successfully. If you're unsure, ask your manager, "When would you need this done by and what would a successful result look like?"

Based on that data, consider your current bandwidth. If a successful result feels unrealistic, ask yourself why. One of the most common reasons may be that you simply have too much on your to-do list to take on the project in the given time frame. (If you have time, spend a day or two tracking how much time you're spending on each item on your current to-do list before answering your manager.)

Once you have a better idea of your bandwidth, find a time to speak to your manager one-on-one and calmly explain your situation, using any data you've gathered to support you. If the task is time sensitive or business critical, and you can't turn around results fast enough, ask your manager to help you reprioritize the responsibilities you've already committed to. You can say: "I'd be happy to take this on, but I'm not able to get it done by the deadline given everything else on my plate. Can you help me reprioritize my to-do list to free up more space in my schedule?"

I've also found that collaboration tools like Trello and Airtable, which allow you to track your current tasks, can help keep you and your manager on the same page by making your workload visible to them. I recommend using these tools to document your pipeline of projects. Then share your pipeline with your manager so that they can see what you're working on before assigning you something new.

–Dviwesh Mehta (he/him), Regional Director, South Asia and the Middle East, Higher Education, Harvard Business Publishing

QUICK RECAP

We are encouraged (and expected) to say yes to everything at work. But ultimately, you won't benefit from taking on tasks you don't have the bandwidth for. Here's how to say no to your boss.

- Take a day to think. Saying yes to tasks outside of your comfort zone can be rewarding, but spreading yourself too thin will hurt your performance.

- Be clear why you're turning a task down. Simply saying no leaves too much room for assumptions.

- Back up your answer with data. Spend a day or two tracking how much time you're spending on each item on your to-do list before deciding whether you have the bandwidth for more.

Adapted from "3 Ways to Say 'No' to Your Boss" on hbr.org, March 9, 2023.

Want to learn more about how to say no at work?
Watch this video from HBR:

How to Deal with a Jealous Manager

by Ruchi Sinha

Comparing ourselves to others is a central part of the human experience. You can see it in almost every stage of life: a toddler who wants a new toy because their buddy got one; a teen searching for the best photo app so their Instagram pictures measure up to those of their friends; or an adult grateful to have spent the lockdown in their apartment with a balcony and great views while their peer was stuck in a windowless studio.

At work, too, comparisons are commonplace. Sometimes we're envious of a colleague's great presentation or jealous that someone else got picked to work on that high-profile project. Sometimes we face jealousy in response to our own successes as well.

But what if the jealousy or resentment is coming from your manager?

When an insecure manager is confronted with a subordinate who outshines them, they are likely to feel threatened. Research shows that in such cases, managers tend to react in a couple of ways:[1]

Reactions that will not hurt you. Your manager finds a way to humbly self-deprecate and believes you perform as well as you do because you're exceptional. This false narrative helps them justify their own comparative shortcomings or lack of popularity.

If this is your situation, your manager is probably harmless, and it's best not to stir the pot.

Reactions that can hurt you. Your manager often says or does things that makes their jealousy evident. Here are some telltale signs that their reactions are harmful:

- They always find something to criticize about your work, even when it drives results and is praised by others.

- They frequently interrupt you during meetings or one-on-ones.

- They belittle your accomplishments in front of your team.

- They ignore you.

- They seem to enjoy pointing out your mistakes.

- They give you projects no one else wants to work on.

If this is your situation, your manager may feel that the recognition you are receiving is unfair or making them look bad. They may see you as a threat and resent you. It's typical for a manager in this mindset to distance themselves from you, socially ostracize you, and attempt to remove any advantages you have in the system. This is not your fault, but it could affect your professional growth and development.

If you're seeing your prospects fade because of a jealous manager, use the following tips to help you manage their emotions (and your career path).

Understand the psychology. Your boss is human and has the same need for status and respect in the workplace as everyone else. When they see you outshining them, they may feel threatened, especially if they perceive their own popularity and status are being diminished. This gives rise to jealousy, envy, or frustration. Psychologists call this the state of *relative deprivation*—feeling disadvantaged or inferior when comparing yourself to others, accompanied by the perception that you are worse off than them.

While it's on your manager to deal with their own feelings of insecurity and resentment, you also might want to check to see if there's anything you need to change about your own behavior. Ask yourself:

- Do I share the spotlight with this person?

- Do I give credit where it is due?

- Do I show enough appreciation and recognition of the teamwork behind my success?

By answering these questions, you will be in a better position to understand if any of your own behaviors have contributed to their insecurities.

Manage their reactions with humility. Inevitably, when we succeed, we attribute the performance to our own ambition, drive, skills, and abilities. Although that might be true, we need to acknowledge the exceptional circumstances and fortunate opportunities we may have received along the way. This is where you can remind your manager about how you are grateful for the support, mentorship, sponsorship, and exposure they may have given you to help you on this path to success. It is critical to do this not just in private conversations but also in front of stakeholders valued by your boss.

For example, the next time your work is honored or called out in a large meeting, you could say, "I also just want to acknowledge that a large part of this success is due to the support of my manager and the opportunities they've given me. I want to specifically thank [manager's name] for encouraging me to take on [opportunity]. This recognition is not just for my performance but for all those decisions they made to make this project happen."

Remember, your humility and gratitude need to be genuine. When appropriate, call out specific events and stories that exemplify your manager's support or talk about how your manager helped you work through a challenge. Thank your manager for exposing you to great networking or development opportunities or giving you a chance to work on high-profile projects.

Use your success to empower both your manager and your peers. When you're prospering, you may become more focused on your own achievements. But it's critical to stop and find ways to use your influence to help others succeed. If you have a certain level of leverage because of your success, share that power first with your manager. Invite them to and include them in critical events. Build their profile when you are seen as the star— that's what makes a team player.

You can also share your expertise with peers through formal or informal mentoring or by running team workshops. Your manager is likely to interpret these behaviors positively and see you as an asset to the team rather than a threat.

Proactively defuse the power and status struggles. If your manager feels threatened by your stardom, they may become more aggressive in how they assert their power and influence during meetings and in front of stakeholders. Understand that when your manager is showing off their power over you, it is likely coming from their own feeling of envy. To defuse the source of that threat, don't push back in a struggle for power and status. Instead, validate your boss by acknowledging their expertise and authority. Remind them that you value their support and the contributions they have made to your success.

You could say, "I understand where you're coming from and appreciate your expertise. In fact, I would love your advice on how to accomplish [this task]. Your knowledge and skills have helped me in the past, and I want to learn from you moving forward." This can instill security and positive efficacy, which will help prevent them from socially ostracizing you.

．　．　．

Don't let your manager's actions frustrate you. If your manager is putting you down, reacting in ways that hurt you, or crowding out your success, know that there are ways to manage their bad behavior and turn their rivalry into allyship.

QUICK RECAP

If you're successful at work, it's not rare for some people to feel envious—but what if the jealous person is your boss? You may be put in the unenviable position where you need to manage *their* emotions to manage your own career.

- **Understand the psychology.** Explore whether and how your actions have contributed to their insecurities.

- **Manage their reactions with humility.** Show how you are grateful for the support they have given you.

- **Use your success to empower others.** Wield your influence to shine a light on the good work of your boss and team members.

- **Proactively defuse the power and status struggles.** Don't reciprocate in the struggle for status. Instead, validate your boss by acknowledging their expertise and authority.

Adapted from content posted on hbr.org, December 18, 2020.

Want to learn more about working with an insecure boss?
Watch this video from HBR:

5

How to Give Negative Feedback to Your Manager

by Nicole D. Smith

Your boss makes decisions about your workload, performance ratings, pay, promotions, and more. That overarching power dynamic means you'll want to be thoughtful about when, how often, and how best to give them negative feedback. Managers are people, and just like everyone else, there are times when they make mistakes or need to develop new skills to perform at their best.

If you deliver your feedback thoughtfully, it could end up strengthening your relationship and even benefiting your growth. Here's the key: It's not just about what you say—it's about how you say it.

Be prepared

Like with all feedback, negative feedback should be specific, especially if you're giving it to your manager. When preparing to share your observation, ask yourself what actions, mistakes, choices, or judgments you want to discuss. Choose what you're going to focus on, stick to it, and plan to be organized in your delivery.

You should be able to explain the problem and how it's impacting you, your team, or the organization. This will help your boss understand their missteps more clearly (without overwhelming them) and help you prepare a criticism that's thoughtful and fair.

Be timely

When delivering negative feedback, timing is everything. Timeliness will inform your boss that there's a problem. Most likely, with the several people and projects that your boss manages, your observations or problems may not be on their radar. Plus, timely feedback can help lessen frustration, confusion, or other feelings you have that you might otherwise be keeping to yourself. That's why sooner is usually better than later. You want the conversation to feel relevant.

Prepare them by setting the stage, but I recommend keeping any specifics for the actual conversation. (You don't want to put them on the defense before you even get a chance to talk.) You might say, "I wanted to discuss how I felt when you were giving instructions during the meeting today. Do you have some time to talk?"

Be constructive, controlled, and respectful

During the meeting with your manager, keep in mind that giving negative feedback can feel uncomfortable, and even intimidating, when it's your boss. Emotions are often a large part of delivering feedback—not only for you but for your boss as well. It's important to be able to control and regulate your emotions during the conversation. If you feel overwhelmed in the moment, take a deep breath, and then deliver.

Try to cover five things: Thank them for being open to listening, and then state your intention in sharing feedback (keep this productive and positive), what you want to see change, why you want to see it change, and any negative impacts you've observed as a result of their actions or behavior.

Be curious

When you've finished sharing negative feedback, prompt your manager to ask questions or share their own perspective. Simple prompts like, "What are your thoughts?" can enable them to openly share, ask for clarity, or reflect out loud. Curious questions can spark an authentic, honest dialogue. You may learn that their behavior wasn't intentional or that they weren't aware of how their actions have been impacting you. Once feedback turns into a conversation, it sets the stage for you both to hear each other, and more importantly, collaborate on possible solutions.

QUICK RECAP

It's uncomfortable and inevitable—sometimes you need to give negative feedback to your boss. When you're having the conversation, it's not just about what you say—it's about how you say it. These tactics can help:

- **Be prepared.** Choose what to focus on, stick to it, and be organized in your delivery.

- **Be timely.** Sooner is usually better than later. You want the conversation to feel relevant.

- **Be constructive, controlled, and respectful.** If you feel overwhelmed in the moment, take a deep breath, and then deliver.

- **Be curious.** Prompt your manager to ask questions or share their own perspective.

Adapted from "How to Give Negative Feedback to Your Peers, Boss, or Direct Reports" on hbr.org, April 11, 2023.

Want to learn more about how to handle a bad boss? Listen to this episode of *New Here* from HBR:

6

How to Have a Successful Meeting with Your Boss's Boss

by Melody Wilding

How well do you know your manager's manager? How much time have you spent with them without your boss present? If you're like most of the professionals I work with, then the answer to both of these questions is probably "very little." And yet managing up doesn't stop at influencing your immediate boss. It also requires that you build relationships with leaders further up your chain of command, including with your "grandmanager" or "big boss."

One of the most effective ways to forge a connection with those above you is through a skip-level meeting—a one-on-one between you and your boss's boss. It's an opportunity to communicate directly with a higher-up whom you may not have much regular access to or interaction with. Having skip-levels ensures that you're not only effective in your role but also aligned, informed, and increasingly visible. They allow you to:

- *Gain a broader perspective.* Interacting directly with your manager's manager helps you align with the company's broader strategic direction and pitch projects and initiatives that resonate with what's valued at the top.

- *Build social capital.* Creating a rapport with your boss's boss lays the foundation for trust, which can prove invaluable during times of change, transitions, and uncertainty.

- *Enhance advocacy.* These meetings provide a platform to showcase accomplishments, request the resources your team needs, and position yourself for further growth.

Here's how to set up, hold, and leverage upward skip-level conversations for your own benefit—and the organization's as a whole.

Consider your culture

For many of the professionals I coach, the thought of interacting directly with their skip-level manager can be intimidating. Self-doubt creeps in and they worry about wasting a senior leader's time or coming off as "trying too hard." These are valid concerns. Navigating a relationship with your manager's manager requires a delicate balance. Overstep, and you might be seen as bypassing your immediate supervisor.

So tread carefully. Before you jump to schedule a skip-level, consider your workplace culture and how such a request would be perceived. Would it be welcomed—or seen as a threat? Some companies encourage open communication, while others may have more hierarchical structures. Reflect on past interactions and feedback from your supervisor. Have they previously encouraged you to take initiative, or have they advised a more cautious approach? This can offer insight into how they might perceive your request.

Bring your boss into the loop

If you do proceed, transparency is key. Choose a private time when you and your immediate supervisor can have a candid conversation. Explain why you believe a skip-level meeting would be beneficial for you and the team as a whole. Perhaps share how it will help you make informed decisions, lessen back-and-forth, or avoid last-minute surprises that use up valuable time and resources. Emphasize that your intention is not to undermine or bypass your manager, but rather to enhance your own understanding and alignment with the organization. Your boss will appreciate understanding the motivation behind your request.

Asking your boss questions like "How would you suggest I maximize the time?" or "Are there specific topics you think would be good for me to cover?" demonstrates that you respect their expertise and positions the request as a collaborative effort. If your boss expresses reservations or suggests waiting for a more opportune moment, listen. They may have insights about workplace politics that you aren't privy to.

Define your goals

You don't want to disrespect your skip-level's time by coming unprepared, so define your objectives in advance. Are you clarifying expectations? Describe your current understanding and ask for affirmation or correction. Seeking guidance? Outline specific challenges or opportunities you're facing and the solution you're leaning toward, and ask how they've dealt with similar situations in the past. Presenting information? Share a clear, concise summary and tailor the data to what would interest an executive, focusing on impact and results.

Prepare powerful questions

Regardless of what you want to get out of the conversation, your primary job is to listen. Follow the 70/30 rule: You should aim to speak 30% of the time and allow your boss's boss to speak for 70% of the time. By listening more, you avail yourself of their experiences and insights and can more easily pick up on nonobvious nuances.

Furthermore, you're forced to be concise and purposeful in your communication. Your speaking time becomes more about asking the right questions—ones that showcase your strategic thinking and derive clarity. For example:

- From your perspective, what do you believe are the most significant challenges our team should be addressing?

- How do you envision our team's role evolving given the company's long-term strategy?

- Based on your observations, how can I grow in my role to better support both our immediate team and the larger organization?

- What trends or changes in the market should we be paying attention to or learning from?

- When you envision our company five or 10 years down the road, what are the key milestones you hope we've achieved?

- Given the challenges our industry faces, what keeps you optimistic?

Build the relationship

Building a genuine, meaningful relationship with anyone—especially your manager's manager—is about consistently demonstrating respect, integrity, and initiative. A little appreciation goes a long way, so always send a follow-up email after the meeting to thank your skip-level boss for their time. You might also summarize key takeaways or share how you plan to act on their guidance.

Accountability matters. If you said you would circle back about a certain point or question, make good on your promise and show you're reliable. Also consider asking for a quarterly meeting and get it on the calendar as soon as possible.

. . .

Taking the time and effort to invest in upward relationships, such as those with skip-level managers, requires strategy, humility, and diligence. After all, leadership is not only about managing those below you, but also navigating the complexities above.

QUICK RECAP

One of the most effective ways to forge upward relationships in your organization is through a skip-level meeting. To have an effective one-on-one with your boss's boss, follow these tips:

- **Consider your culture.** Think about how your manager would perceive you meeting with their manager.

- **Bring your boss into the loop.** If you do proceed, transparency is key.

- **Define your goals.** Don't disrespect your skip-level's time by coming unprepared.

- **Prepare powerful questions.** Be concise and purposeful in your communication.

- **Build the relationship.** Thank them and follow up on any points that came up in the meeting.

Adapted from content posted on hbr.org, September 19, 2023.

Coworkers, Teammates, and Work Friends

Three Types of Difficult Coworkers and How to Work with Them

by Amy Gallo

In every workplace, there are people—many of whom have earned respect and positions of power—who behave in ways that are thoughtless, ambiguous, irrational, and even sometimes downright malicious.

It can be challenging to know exactly how to work with people who act like this. Odds are, no one has sat you down and said, "Here's how you push back on an aggressive know-it-all," or "Try this approach for dealing with an incessant naysayer." You likely never took a class on handling a colleague who plays dirty office politics or had a mentor share advice on what to do if you find yourself working for an incompetent boss.

However, when we don't address these small conflicts with our coworkers, the stress can affect our productivity, make work miserable, and even bleed into other aspects of our lives. That's why it's important to learn why challenging colleagues behave the way they do, master tactics for dealing with their most difficult traits, and ultimately decide when to persist in our efforts or to walk away.

Building a relationship with a difficult colleague may seem hard, but it's a skill you can learn. Here are three common archetypes of difficult coworkers, the behaviors they often exhibit, and how you can manage your relationship with them.

The Pessimist

What it looks like

The more Simran allowed her colleague Theresa to vent her concerns about the company and her life, the more time Theresa spent complaining to her. Theresa couldn't seem to find anything positive to say—ever—and even seemed to enjoy coming up with all the different ways a project or initiative could fail. For Simran, Theresa's griping was becoming a physical and psychological drain.

Why it happens

There are a lot of reasons why pessimists think and behave the way they do. A pessimist could be motivated by anxiety, a desire for power, or resentment about how they've been treated in the past. Still, some might have legitimate reasons for being negative. For example, during the launch of a new product, they might articulate risks related to getting customers to buy into the new idea or point out workplace issues that most people are refusing to acknowledge or notice.

Regardless of why a pessimist acts the way they do, it's important to find ways to work productively with them. After all, negative attitudes can be contagious, infecting not just you but the whole team.

Tactics to try

- *Acknowledge their complaints; then reframe them.* For instance, if the pessimist grumbles that another team member is lazy, say something like, "It's a busy time for everyone. I bet they're doing more than we can see." Don't be patronizing, or mean, but present an alternative view. You can also ask your colleague to be constructive. For example, you could say, "I can see why you're frustrated. Do you think there's anything we can do?" Or "What could we try next time?" The goal is to increase the cynic's sense of agency by pointing out actions they can take or even telling a story of a time when you encountered similar circumstances and responded productively.

- *Use their outlook as a positive tool.* If your colleague is a natural at pointing out risks, perhaps that can be part of their formal role. You've undoubtedly heard the advice to appoint a "devil's advocate" who is tasked with raising difficult questions and challenging a group's thinking.

Research shows that giving at least one person the right to push back in this way leads to better decision-making for the team as a whole.[1] If you're their manager, you can ask them to play this role. If you're not, consider seeking out your colleague's perspective when you need a more critical eye on a project you're working on or a decision you're making.

- *Agree to team norms.* Although singling people out is sometimes counterproductive, you can set norms for the whole team that will nudge a killjoy in the right direction. For example, you could agree as a group that everyone will ask themselves before they speak, "Will this comment be helpful?" You might also agree that criticism should be accompanied by a suggestion of what to do instead.

Some phrases to use with a pessimist

- "What would need to be true for us to succeed?"

- "If you're unhappy with (person, leader, project), let's discuss what steps you can take to change the situation. I have some ideas, but I'd love to hear your thoughts first."

- "There's a part of me that agrees with you that this might not work. And another part of me thinks it will. Let's tease out both perspectives."

- "You're good at identifying the downsides. What might we be missing here?"

The Passive-Aggressive Peer

What it looks like

Malik was at his wits' end with his coworker Susan, who would act like she was on board with a decision in a meeting but then drop the ball and deflect the blame toward him. Susan would often say one thing but do another, display negative body language but insist everything was "fine," and deliver insults that sounded like compliments.

Why it happens

Gabrielle Adams, a professor at the University of Virginia who studies interpersonal conflict at work, defines *passive-aggressive* as not being forthcoming about what you're truly thinking and using indirect methods to express your thoughts and feelings. Often, it's driven by the fear of failure or rejection, a desire to avoid conflict, or a feeling of powerlessness.

Tactics to try

- *Avoid labeling them as passive-aggressive.* It's tempting to call out the behavior directly. But saying "Stop being so passive-aggressive" will only make things worse. It's a loaded phrase, and it's rare that someone will be willing to acknowledge or own up to it. More likely, calling them out will only make them angrier and more defensive. Instead, try using strategies that help you understand their perspective better.

- *Focus on the underlying message, not their behavior.* Seek to understand what your colleague is really trying to say. What is the underlying idea they're attempting to convey (even if it's wrapped up in a snarky comment)? Do they think that the way you're running a project isn't working? Or do they disagree about the team's goals? Remember that not everyone feels comfortable discussing their thoughts and opinions openly. If you can focus on your coworker's underlying concern or question rather than the way they're expressing themselves, you may be able to address the actual problem.

- *Create a safe environment for an honest conversation.* Social psychologist Heidi Grant told me, in an interview for my book *Getting Along*, that the best tactic is to show interest in the other person's perspective, no matter how hard it may be for you to hear. You might say, "I heard your views during the meeting and interpreted it as. . . . Did I get it right?" The advantage to opening up a conversation is that it allows the person to label their own behavior and emotions. If your colleague acknowledges how they're actually feeling (although there's no guarantee that they will), they are one step closer to breaking the habit of responding passive-aggressively.

Some phrases to use with a passive-aggressive peer

- "I heard you say [quick summary], but I wasn't sure if you meant something else. Is there something I'm not understanding?"

- "I noticed that you pushed away from the table (or rolled your eyes). What's your reaction to this discussion?"

- "I've noticed that you haven't been responding to my emails. Is there something wrong? I don't mean to pry, but just want to be sure everything's OK."

The Know-It-All

What it looks like

Lucia's colleague Ray loved to talk. If people tried to interrupt him, he just raised his voice and spoke over them. Lucia interpreted his diatribes as Ray saying, "I know what the team and company need, and everyone else should just listen." Ray seemed convinced that he was the smartest person in the room, and he loved telling people what was "right," even when he was clearly wrong.

Why it happens

Confidence can be a good thing, but confidence without competence can cause people to ignore feedback, act condescendingly, and take credit for group successes. Some know-it-alls have adopted this behavior to compensate for feelings of insecurity. For others, it has been encouraged by corporate norms. Either way, know-it-alls can undermine team cohesiveness and demean you to the point of damaging your career.

Tactics to try

- *Address interruptions.* One way to avoid interruptions is to preemptively request that people refrain from interjecting. Before you start talking, explain how much time (roughly) you're going to need and say something like, "Please hold any comments or questions until I'm done." If you're not making a formal presentation but are just having a discussion where some back-and-forth is expected, you might say instead, "Interruptions break my concentration, so I'd appreciate it if I could finish my thoughts before you jump in." If your efforts to preempt interruptions fail, address them directly. But don't just raise your voice. That sets up a power struggle and your colleague is likely to talk louder in an attempt to drown you out. Instead, confidently say, "I'm going to finish my point, and then I'd love to hear what you have to say."

- *Ask for specific facts.* Another habit of the know-it-all is to proclaim things they have no way of knowing for sure, like "In a year, no one will even be talking about this recession." When this happens, understand that it's OK to ask people for sources or data that back up their declarations. Be respectful, not confrontational. You might say something like, "I'm not sure we're working with the same assumptions and facts. Let's step back and take a look at the data before we proceed." If you don't have data, you might even suggest you all gather some. For instance, if your colleague insists that customers will hate a new product feature, is it feasible to run a short customer survey?

- *Model humility.* Many show-offs act the way they do because, implicitly or explicitly, they've received messages that projecting confidence is what's expected on your team, in your organization, or in the culture they're from. You can provide a different model by displaying humility and open-mindedness. Try saying, "I don't know" or "I don't have that information right now; let me get back to you." If the know-it-all sees that you suffer no consequences for expressing uncertainty, they may be willing to do the same.

Some phrases to use with a know-it-all

- "I'd appreciate it if you would respect that I know what I'm doing. I value your input, and I'll definitely ask for it when I need it."

- "Interruptions break my concentration, so I'd appreciate it if you'd let me finish my thoughts before jumping in."

- "I'm going to continue, and I'll address that when I'm done."

- "Tell me about where your insights are coming from."

. . .

Much of the advice here requires you to be "the adult in the room." And you may be wondering why you should do all the work if your colleague is the one causing the problems. Truthfully, it's not on you to change another person's behavior, and oftentimes, you can't. What you can change is your approach to navigating relationships that are critical in your work life. You may notice that sometimes trying something new, even something small, can shift the dynamic between you and a coworker who gets under your skin. Hopefully, with this advice, you'll be able to more easily put work conflict in its place, freeing up valuable time and mental capacity for the things that really matter to you.

QUICK RECAP

Building a relationship with a difficult colleague may seem hard, but it's a skill you can learn. Sometimes trying something new, even something small, can shift the dynamic between you and a coworker who gets under your skin:

- If you're dealing with a pessimist, try acknowledging and reframing their complaints, using their outlook as a positive tool, and agreeing to team norms.

- If you're dealing with a passive-aggressive peer, avoid the label "passive-aggressive." Try focusing on their underlying message and making space for an honest conversation.

- If you're dealing with a know-it-all, try addressing their interruptions, asking for specific facts, and modeling humility.

Adapted from "3 Types of Difficult Coworkers and How to Work with Them" on hbr.org, May 30, 2023.

Want to learn more about working with a passive-aggressive peer?
Watch this video from HBR:

New to the Team? Here's How to Build Trust (Remotely)

by Ruchi Sinha

Trust isn't easy to build. It develops slowly, typically after you and another person have been able to interact and assess each other's characters. If all goes well, you start to feel psychologically safe and that you can rely on one another. But remote work has made this process difficult.

Many of us now interact on-screen and work on hybrid teams with people located around the world. We lack the luxury of regularly observing our peers in person, making it harder to gauge their intentions, values, and characters (and vice versa).

This is a problem. In any kind of work environment, you need trust for all kinds of reasons. Without it, you may not feel comfortable bringing your full self to work. You and your teammates may struggle to support one another or openly share ideas and opinions, leading to damaging miscommunications, decreased productivity, and a fear of taking risks that could help you learn and grow in your career.

As an academic, I have explored trust in many different contexts, including how it is rebuilt in the aftermath of conflict and how the emotions we express during negotiations impact trust. Through my own work, as well as extensive reading, I've learned that how we judge trustworthiness of others is fundamentally the same, no matter what the type of relationship. There are ways to build and sustain trust if you know how to send and receive the right signals.

Competence, integrity, and benevolence are three of the most readable indicators of trust.[1] The good news is you can display them whether you are in person or remote, and you can encourage them on your team.

Competence

Competence is your ability to do something efficiently and successfully. When others perceive you as competent, they believe that you have the skills and knowledge to do what you say you will. This allows them to perceive you as dependable, reliable, and predictable—all of which are essential drivers of trust. Some things you can do to signal your competence include:

- *Be organized and planful.* Before team meetings, do your homework and study the agenda. Show up with a list of questions, research, or solutions that may be of interest to the stakeholders involved in the project. Your peers will see that you are a prepared, motivated, and organized team player.

- *Show reliability and consistency.* Be consistent in the messages you give out. If you've said no to meeting a deadline to one team member, don't switch to a yes when another member asks. If you have critical feedback on a project, don't tell one coworker and hide your concerns from another. People inherently associate consistency and commitment with dependability. Treat everyone fairly and make sure your behaviors match your values.

- *Be thoughtful about what you promise.* Don't promise things that you don't have the time or motivation to deliver on. Avoid overpromising and underdelivering (like agreeing to a deadline that is two days away when realistically it will take you a week to get things done). When talking to teammates, avoid making generic statements of support ("Yeah, good idea. We should do something about that."). Instead, offer actionable ways in which you can support them when you like their ideas ("Hey, I love that idea. I'm happy to help you write out an action plan next week."). Likewise, if you don't agree with an idea, be honest and don't give inauthentic support just for the sake of avoiding a difficult conversation.

- *Be predictable and dependable.* Create transparency around your actions by explaining your motives, values, and criteria. For example, when you suggest ideas to your colleagues, you can say, "Here's what I think we should do. Let's focus on doing X. The reason I'm suggesting this is because I've considered factors A, B and C. Here are my assumptions and rationale for picking X over other options. I'm open to feedback and would love you to weigh in on the best path forward."

Benevolence

Benevolence is the quality of being well-meaning and having others' interests at heart. Other will grow to trust you based on the extent to which they believe you care about their interests and are willing to go beyond your own needs to make sure that the needs of your team are being met. Some things you can do to signal your benevolence include:

- *Identify similarities.* People will be more open to your ideas if they feel your values overlap with theirs. Try to identify the ideas and goals you and your teammates share by engaging them in genuine conversations. For example, when someone shares a detail about their life at the start of a meeting, try to relate to them by sharing something of your own. When someone asks how you're doing, take it as an opportunity to engage authentically. Be honest about the challenges and struggles you are facing—and ask questions back. Finally, when talking about your ideas, link them to your values. This will give others a chance to make deeper connections with you. The more your peers understand where you are coming from, the more likely they will be to support you.

- *Show kindness and compassion.* Small gestures make a big difference. During informal catch-ups or conversations on Slack or IM, take the time to ask your teammates how they are feeling—and be genuinely interested. People will likely see you as someone who cares about others. For example, you could pitch in to help a colleague who is struggling with a family emergency or give a shout-out to your colleague's work at the next team meeting. When others see you as someone who shows kindness and compassion, they are more likely to interpret what you say in a positive light and believe you are more trustworthy.

- *Show restraint.* Be careful about the words you choose. During meetings, make sure your comments are not dismissive. Avoid scoffing and eyerolls, no matter how uninterested you may be. Don't dominate the conversation; instead, make sure everyone gets a chance to speak. And avoid gossiping: If a teammate has shared personal information with you, it's not your place to share it with others. You need to care about privacy at work. Be mindful of managing personal and professional boundaries so that you can be trusted with sensitive information.

Integrity

Integrity is how strongly you adhere to moral principles and how honest you are. Integrity is hard to judge, but it's critical for trust building. A lot of behaviors at work are seen as instrumental and strategic, so people can be unsure about whether your actions are based on sincere values or merely a facade. The more opportunities you have to articulate your values explicitly and to allow team members to see them in action, the more likely they will be to invest their trust in you.

- *Show loyalty.* Find ways to show your support and allegiance to your team members. As a new member, you can show loyalty by endorsing the reputation of your team to external parties, defending its vision and mission, and acting in the interest of the team goals rather than your personal goals. If your manager praises you for a presentation you developed with three other team members, give credit where it's due. Instead of saying, "Thank you, I worked hard on it," you can say, "Thank you. I'd like to acknowledge all the help I received from X, Y, and Z."

- *Listen.* By listening to and considering your teammates' perspectives before you make decisions, you show that you are reflective and deliberate, as opposed to impulsive and indifferent. For example, if you find yourself in a disagreement, instead of posing a counterargument, first take the time to listen to your colleague. Try and understand their side of the discussion. Ask clarifying questions and then make your point. You could say, "The way I see it, you mean X." This shows that you listened to their points and that you want to understand them before you react—and not just win the argument for the sake of winning.

- *Show "citizenship."* Try to go beyond your duties to personally do better than what is expected of you, and to help others achieve excellence. For example, you could take the initiative to act in prosocial ways by offering to teach skills that can improve your colleagues' performance at work. Are you a pro at Excel? Lead a mini master class for your peers.

. . .

Successful teams are made of successful teamwork, and for that, trust is key. Show your coworkers that you're worthy of their trust by displaying competence, integrity, and benevolence. Be consistent, and look for consistency in the actions of your peers. That's how they'll develop stable beliefs about your character and how you can measure whether or not it's worth investing your time and trust in them.

QUICK RECAP

Remote and hybrid work arrangements can make it harder to read your coworkers' intentions, values, and characters. To build trust, especially if you're new to a team, start by displaying three key indicators of trust—and looking for them in your team members.

- **Competence.** When others see you as competent, they believe that you have the skills and knowledge to do what you say you will.

- **Benevolence.** People will trust you based on how much they believe you care about their interests and are willing to make sure the team's needs are being met.

- **Integrity.** Seek opportunities where you can act in line with your values so that others become aware of your inclinations.

Adapted from content posted on hbr.org, March 23, 2021.

Want to learn more about building and repairing trust at work?
Watch this video from HBR:

9

How to Make Friends Across Age Gaps at Work

by Jeff Tan

When I interviewed for my first job, I was focused solely on impressing the hiring managers. Getting an offer was the priority, and everything else came second. What I didn't think about was what life would be like after I landed the role. It wasn't until much later that I realized how important the connections I'd formed with my coworkers had become. Not only did they provide me with community, they also made me a better employee.

Today's younger workers appear to be a bit more in tune with what they want in a job (beyond the role and the salary) than I was in my early career. In a recent survey of more than 200 Gen Zers, participants reported that having a sense of community (along with paid time off and mental health days) is essential to them at work—something it took me several years to value.[1]

At the same time, new grads beginning their first jobs may find that a strong "community" is not so easy to form. The workforce now famously holds five generations, and if you're just entering it, you're likely joining a company with people much older than you are.

Some of your coworkers may be well established in their careers. Others may be in completely different stages of their lives—getting married, starting families, or buying their first homes. Not everyone is heading the same direction. Not everyone is invested in building relationships with their peers.

But don't be discouraged. There are incredible opportunities for mentorship and friendship if you seek out the ones who are interested.

To successfully build relationships with older coworkers, try a few of the methods that have worked for me throughout my career. You can apply them before deciding if an organization is right for you, or use them to form deeper bonds with your colleagues after accepting a role.

Vet the team dynamic during the interview process

The first step to building strong relationships at work is ensuring that the company culture is designed to foster them. Asking the right questions during the interview process can reveal a lot.

To prepare, spend some time beforehand reflecting on the positive and negative learnings or work experiences you've had in the past. What kind of relationships did you value most? Will you be able to form them on your new team? Write down a few direct questions, being as intentional and specific as possible.

When I decided to leave my first job as a life sciences strategy consultant, for example, I spent some time reflecting on what was and wasn't important to me at work. I took stock of all the relationships I had cultivated and discovered that I was willing to work much harder and much longer to support the people I had the strongest connections with. I remember taking on an additional project and carving time out of my weekend to support a manager who had become a mentor to me. I didn't have to take on the project, but I wanted to support her. That, along with the extra experience and exposure, made it worth it.

Knowing this, I was able to seek out a similar experience in my next position by asking questions resembling the following:

- What's your leadership philosophy? Or, What's most valuable to you as a manager?

- What kind of resources have you invested in to help cultivate a positive team dynamic?

- Do you (or does your boss) value relationship-building across all age groups?

- Does your company have a mentorship program?

- In your opinion, how does forming strong connections with your coworkers impact performance?

Listen carefully to the responses. You can determine for yourself if their answers go beyond the generalities and really align with your needs. Do they realize the many benefits of camaraderie to team performance? Even if their answers are not perfect, you may see potential.

Create opportunities to connect with older coworkers

What if you already accepted an offer? How can you start off on good footing with senior colleagues?

The first step is having the right mindset. It's easy to dismiss cross-generational relationships, to believe that we can't connect with people older than ourselves. After all, we come from different generations. We have experiences that result in our varied priorities, beliefs, and values.

Moreover, the more seasoned a colleague is, the more influence and power they likely hold. You may feel an added layer of pressure to appear knowledgeable or impressive when speaking with them. This can be intimidating, but don't limit your interactions to surface-level or transactional conversations. You might not realize it, but your older coworkers may be equally intimidated by you.

Try using the suggestions below to help you move past these feelings:

Think of your older coworkers as more-senior peers. Viewing your coworkers as peers helps to shift your inner narrative and take away some of the pressure you may feel to impress them. When you change your perspective in this way, you may find it easier to be authentic and initiate more organic discussions. Though how you relate to each person will vary, I've personally found that sharing a sense of humor helps. That said, to avoid coming off too strong, the best way to begin is by asking questions: How did they end up in their current role? What hobbies interest them? Simple conversation starters can help you identify common ground.

Set up regular one-on-ones (biweekly, monthly, or quarterly). A monthly coffee or a virtual catch-up is a great way to get to know someone on a personal level. Just be careful not to overshare too soon. Sometimes we think that sharing can help fast-track a connection, but in the work setting, it's usually better to let the level of comfort grow over time. After forming a foundation of trust, however, you can use these opportunities to exchange ideas, and even inspire one another. Once you both become more engaged, your relationship may become mutually beneficial at work (and beyond).

Listen diligently when they speak. The idea here is to remember the topics, interests, and values that are important to your colleague—just like you would with an important friend. This shows that you care about them and are genuinely invested. It's hard to remember all the details, so if you need to jot things down onto a notepad to remind yourself for future conversations, do it!

Know that not everyone is going to be your friend

Try not to be disappointed if you don't naturally connect with someone you admire. Just like in life, you are going to connect with certain people better than others at work. You may end up building office friendships with a select few and have more professional working relationships with the rest. These aren't mutually exclusive, but it can be helpful to understand the difference.

- *Office friendships* are usually rooted in shared personal interests and can nurture a sense of community and belonging at work. For instance, I became great friends with an administrative assistant in my last job. This person later became a mentor—not in a professional sense, but in a personal one. They passed down life lessons that continue to shape who I am today.

- *Working relationships* tend to be rooted in shared professional interests and can help with your career development. An example that comes to mind is the strong working relationship I developed with a marketer at my former company. This person is a cancer survivor, and we connected over our passion to get our newest pharmaceutical drug to market. My mother was a cancer survivor as well, so we were both adamant about helping as many cancer patients as possible. Our relationship led to many professional opportunities that advanced my career.

Both types of relationships are valuable and worth pursuing.

Ask for advice and invest in developing mentors

Many senior employees enjoy mentorship. For them, passing down the lessons they have learned throughout their careers is a reward in itself. Once you've comfortably settled into your new role and have made some connections, start to leverage the most meaningful ones to your benefit.

Think of your senior colleagues as resources who can help you solve the problems you're facing at work. Ask them how they would approach situations you find challenging. Those who are enthusiastic to share their advice may have mentor—or perhaps sponsor—potential. A mentor or sponsor won't just help you develop professionally. You also need advocates in senior roles to build influence and social capital within your organization.

. . .

Though taking these steps may feel overwhelming or intimidating initially, stick with it. Sometimes, the challenge of forming connections at work can become so big that we feel isolated and even consider leaving our jobs. In the end, you can't force a relationship. You are going to meet coworkers, especially older ones, who are not going to be as interested in connecting as you are. But there will also be people who are willing to make the effort, and those relationships can be life-changing. Pursue them.

QUICK RECAP

It can be challenging to connect with coworkers who are older or at different stages of their professional lives. But strengthening these relationships can lead to a more fulfilling work environment, provide opportunities, and make you better at your job. Try these strategies:

- When interviewing for a new position, ask questions to learn about the team's view on age dynamics and culture.

- Reframe your view on relationships with older coworkers and create opportunities to connect. Think of them as older peers, set up one-on-ones, and listen.

- Recognize that work friendships and working relationships are different and can both be valuable.

- Ask for advice and invest in developing advocates.

Adapted from content posted on hbr.org, November 29, 2021.

Want to learn more about why work friends are worth it?
Listen to this episode of *HBR IdeaCast:*

10

Yes, It's Possible to (Gracefully) Talk Politics at Work

by Raina Brands

Several years ago, ABC News released a music video by Will.I.Am aimed at increasing the voter turnout for the 2008 U.S. presidential election.[1] The video, "Yes We Can," quickly went viral and became a rallying call for those supporting Barack Obama's campaign.

Two of my coworkers had very different reactions to the video. Emma stepped into my office at the end of a long day and breathlessly described how she'd been listening to the song on repeat. It had inspired her to seriously consider quitting her job to campaign for Obama full-time. The next day, I saw another coworker, Logan, arguing passionately with Emma about the video. "It's all editing and music," he yelled. "Where's the message of substance?" Emma rolled her eyes and walked away.

At the time, I was shocked that a music video could produce such a strong emotional argument between two of my peers. But as political divides across the world widen, these kinds of conflicts are becoming more common.

You may have had disagreements with your coworkers over tasks, how you should respond to a client, or what next steps to take in a project. But at the end of the day, work is work, and it's usually not personal.

Political conflicts, on the other hand, are personal. They tend to challenge our values and upset our sense of emotional balance.

You've likely heard the expressions "The enemy of my enemy is my friend," or "A friend of my friend is a friend." These sayings are drawn from *balance theory*, which explains how mutual agreement on feelings, attitudes, and beliefs can lead to the formation of positive relationships. But the expression "A friend of my friend is a friend" doesn't just apply to other people; it applies to social objects—like values—as well.

For example, if you strongly identify as politically liberal, you may find that many of your friends are liberal, too, and vice versa. So if you find out that a coworker you like disagrees with one of your strongly identified values, it causes a great deal of emotional tension. We know from studies of social relationships that we resolve this tension in one of two ways—either we change our values or we change our relationships.[2] Neither of those outcomes is desirable in the workplace, because you have to be able to work well with all kinds of people despite divergent beliefs.

Assuming that we want to hold on to our core values at work *and* maintain good working relationships, what can we do?

The answer is surprisingly simple: Have a conversation. It won't always be easy, but rest assured, there are ways to gracefully navigate a debate about politics at work.

Start by listening. When our values are challenged, it's hard to resist the urge to speak out and "correct" others' views. However, a more productive approach is to start by listening to your coworker. I don't just mean waiting for them to finish talking before you share your point of view. I mean fully *exploring* their point of view. Ask open questions (for example, those that start with how, what, why). It is important to express interest, so try using phrases like:

- I've never thought about this perspective before. Can you tell me more?

- I can see you feel strongly about this. Why is this issue important to you?

- That's an interesting thought. How did you arrive at this view?

When you have explored their view, summarize what you've heard to check that you've understood them correctly. The idea here is to paraphrase what they said, not to necessarily agree with them (for example, "Let me see if I understand. You believe . . .").

Listening, of course, is hard to do when your values are challenged, but taking this approach sets the tone for the rest of the conversation. By listening, you send the message that their view is valid (even if you don't agree with it) and you build a norm for interacting that will encourage them to listen and explore your point of view in return.

Reframe the issues that are important to you. Hopefully, now that you've really listened to your coworker, you understand their values. This is essential if you ever want to change their point of view (if that is your goal). When we try to convince other people of our ideas, we often frame our arguments through the lens of our own values. But when people don't share our beliefs, they won't be convinced by arguments built on them. Research shows that when partisan issues are reframed through values that opposing groups care about, those groups increase their support.[3]

This approach can work for you, too. For example in the United States, Democrats and Republicans frequently disagree on military spending. Republicans have traditionally advocated for the expansion of the military, arguing that the military unifies American society and ensures that the United States maintains its standing on the world stage. Democrats tend to disagree, seeing this justification as overly hawkish. Yet when military spending is framed as providing opportunities for social mobility for individuals from disadvantaged backgrounds, Democrats increase their support for military spending.[4]

End on agreement. Now that you have reframed the issue through the lens of each other's values, explore any areas of agreement you share. For example, you might both agree that access to health care should be expanded (even if you disagree on how) and that any candidate for political office who intends to reduce access to health care is unlikely to receive either of your votes. Again, simple phrases like "It sounds like we agree on . . ." or "The overlap between our views is . . ." are all that are needed.

Ending on agreement is important for restoring the sense of emotional balance you feel toward the other person and de-escalating any tension between you. It is unlikely you will leave the conversation having resolved all of your differences. But by finding *some* point of agreement, you will leave the talk on a common ground and leave room for another collaborative conversation in the future.

Remember that there is also a caveat here: Different types of political conversations can happen in the workplace. The types of conversations I've outlined above may make us upset and angry, but they don't threaten our existence or comfort at work. However, other conversations can become hostile or disrespectful to you or your BIPOC or LGBTQIA colleagues. If that is the case, you should initiate a conversation with your manager or HR.

. . .

On the whole, diversity of values, thought, and opinion is an essential part of today's workplace. Engaging with people who hold deeply different views than us can spark new ideas and insights. But this potential is lost when diversity of values breeds misunderstanding and conflict. Ultimately, the responsibility for forging productive working relationships with people with different values falls to the individual, and it starts with a conversation.

QUICK RECAP

As political divides across the world widen, conflicts among colleagues have become more common. If you disagree with a coworker's political beliefs, it's important not to let that negatively impact your working relationship. To do so without compromising your values, have conversations with them.

- Begin the conversation by listening to your coworker and exploring their point of view.

- If your goal is to change your coworker's mind, make sure to reframe the issue in a way they will relate to.

- End the conversation on agreement, leaving open the opportunity for more collaborative discussions in the future.

Adapted from content posted on hbr.org, October 30, 2020.

Want to learn more about how to disagree with someone more powerful than you? Watch this video from HBR:

11

You Can't Sit Out Office Politics

by Niven Postma

For more than two decades, I worked as an executive across the corporate, nonprofit, and public sectors. Throughout these years, I wore my refusal to engage in office politics as a badge of honor. To anyone who would listen (and perhaps even a few who wouldn't), I said, "I really don't have the stomach for all of that stuff. Politics are dreadful, dangerous, and unnecessary, and I'm simply too straightforward for all of the subterfuge they require. I don't come to work to play games—I come to work to get things done."

Given my approach, it's unsurprising that I was entirely unprepared and out of my depth when, several years into my career, I was laid off. It wasn't because I was performing poorly or failing to meet my goals. It was because I had neglected to form relationships with people who had the power to advocate for my job.

I was let go under the guise of budget cuts, but in reality, I had been gracefully and expensively fired without question or reproach because someone with authority wanted me gone. This is an example of office politics at their worst.

The experience made me realize that my head-in-the-sand approach needed updating. It was high time I became a little more *politically* intelligent at work. I immersed myself in the topic. I read every article, book, and study I could lay my hands on and sought professional guidance from a fellow executive-turned-coach.

The more I learned, the more I began to reflect on my career. Though I achieved a great deal of success, there were also many opportunities I had missed and many times that I had faltered as a result of my lack of education around office politics. It's not a subject covered in most colleges or business schools, despite the fact that it's essential to surviving (and thriving) in every work environment.

That's why, in my work now as a global consultant, I've made it a priority to educate professionals at every stage in their careers on organizational politics and how to navigate them at work.

Understanding the Myths

Despite all the negative connotations, office politics are not inherently evil. They are about two things: influence and relationships, and the power these two things give you—or don't. Having now lectured about organizational politics to thousands of employees around the world, I have uncovered five myths that are as widespread and harmful as they are naive and as universal as they are wrong. If you're starting out in your career and think it's best to sit politics out, you should learn the truth sooner than later.

Myth 1: You can either be a good person,
or you can play politics

In every lecture or workshop I run, I start by asking people to use three words to describe office politics. In every case, 99% of the words given are negative. *Toxic, frustrating, dangerous, demotivating, draining, unfair, unnecessary, cliques,* and *gossip* almost always rise to the surface. Last week, an employee used the word *heartbreaking.*

The fact that these are the words we associate with office politics explains why this first myth is so prevalent. How could any of us possibly engage in things that are widely seen as toxic and dangerous, or at the very least unethical and unpleasant, if we are not ourselves toxic, dangerous, unethical, and unpleasant?

This myth is premised on an incomplete and one-sided understanding of what office politics really are. Though office politics can be used both ethically and unethically, at their core they are just the range of informal, unofficial, and sometimes behind-the-scenes efforts that happen in all organizations as people position themselves, their interests, their teams, and their priorities to get things done.

For example, let's say you have a big meeting coming up where stakeholders at your company are going to decide which projects to invest in—including yours. If you're savvy at politics, you know that to get your project approved, you first need to understand the priorities and perspectives of those stakeholders. You need to engage with them beforehand and learn what they are looking for so that you can more persuasively present your idea.

This is an example of how office politics can be ethically used to help you gain an advantage.

Even so, destructive and negative politics also can—and do—exist. In the same situation, if you were to spread a rumor about the lack of scientific evidence behind your colleague's project in order to get yours chosen over theirs, that would be an unethical use of politics.

By painting all political activities with the same brush, we are oblivious to the potential for constructive politics—that is, the range of perfectly ethical and appropriate activities that serve to strengthen relationships of support, expand influence, and build a powerful base that allows you and your team to be more effective.

Myth 2: You can escape office politics

Organizational politics are inescapable. A few years ago, I was sharing this reality with a group of young managers. One of them was visibly concerned by what I was saying, and so I asked him to share what he was thinking.

"I'm really struggling to accept that there is never going to be a place where I am not going to have to deal with politics. Surely there has to be somewhere?"

"Like where?" I asked.

"Well, what about NGOs? Or a church? You know—places where people work for the greater good of the world. Surely there are no politics there?"

I suppressed a laugh and by way of an answer told him the story of a friend of mine who had been a church minister. After having led a congregation for about 10 years, she decided to get into business. The one thing that really concerned her in making the transition was the dreaded "corporate politics" that colleagues warned her about and that friends in business repeatedly complained about. Undeterred, but still quite nervous, she made the leap into a big auditing firm, and after a few months I couldn't wait to find out how it was going.

"I'm loving it," she told me over coffee.

"What about the politics? Are you coping?" I asked her.

"Politics? Are you kidding me? Corporate politics are absolutely *nothing* compared to church politics!"

In their book *Reframing Organizations*, Lee G. Bolman and Terrence E. Deal hit the nail on the head when they state, "The question is not whether organizations will have politics but rather what kind of politics they will have."[1] As human beings, we are social creatures and the use of relationships, informal influence, and power plays is part of how we engage—for better or for worse.

Myth 3: Politics don't affect your job performance or career

How many times have you heard someone say, or perhaps even found yourself saying, "I don't do politics. My work should speak for itself." Carla Harris, vice chairman at Morgan Stanley, has a saying I like better: "You can't let your work speak for you; work doesn't speak."

Since it is people who speak, we need to speak about our work, and we need other people to speak about it, too. However, speaking about our work doesn't mean reciting a laundry list of things that we're doing. Instead, it's about framing what we are doing in terms of the impact it's having on the organization and why it matters.

In workshops and lectures, participants and I often have lengthy discussions about whether self-promotion is necessary, or even desirable. Many of us have a deeply held view that talent and hard work *should* be all that one needs to succeed. I think what lies at the heart of this belief is that so many of us treat work like school. When we are at school, it is generally a given that if we work hard and master the subject material, we will get good marks and proceed to the next level. In the workplace though, thinking like this is a risk and a mistake because the reality at work is that invisible contributions have no value.

Myth 4: Politics disappear in virtual environments

In the absence of in-person interactions, surely all the power play and informal maneuvering tactics employed in office politics disappear? Anyone who has worked remotely knows that this is not the case.

While research shows that office politics diminish in online environments, there's no evidence that they disappear entirely.[2] This isn't surprising—most human beings are much more driven by the informal and political than they are by the formal and prescribed. Again, this can either be negative or positive, but it is a key part of human behavior, no matter what kind of environment we are operating in.

People who think they don't play politics are often very surprised to hear that when they are taking something offline, socializing their idea with decision-makers in advance of a more formal meeting, or just having a chat with someone they think can help them to be more effective, they are in fact engaging in political activities. This is true whether you are doing these things in person or remotely.

Myth 5: Political intelligence is an inherent trait

I am often asked whether certain people are more suited to politics than others. My reply is always the same—the skills that lie at the heart of political intelligence certainly come more naturally to some than to others. But they are still skills. They are not traits that we are either born with or not born with. As with all skills, you need to practice them to master them.

After discussing the key skills and strategies of the politically savvy in one of my workshops, a young manager who was looking at me with a mixture of exhaustion and astonishment, sputtered out, "But this is a lot of work!"

She was spot-on.

With all the demands on your time and energy, it may feel like getting your unread emails down to double figures is the biggest achievement you've made all week. Now, you may be wondering: Am I telling you that, in addition, you need to find the time and energy to invest in relationships, get strategic about your supporters and sponsors, look for ways to increase the influence and power you have, and then use all those things to advance your career?

Well, yes.

Doing so takes intentionality, focus, and practice—and it will come more naturally, second nature even, with time. The alternative (for example, failing to curate your network, build your brand, and all the other things that politically smart people do) is likely to result in an otherwise promising career never reaching the heights that it could. Or even worse, derail your career completely.

What You Can Do

Now that you understand the truth behind these myths, let's take a look at what you can do to ease yourself into playing office politics well.

Reframe what "politics" means to you

Start to be aware of your language and how it is framing your reality, specifically how it frames the way you understand the work environment and how you choose to show up in it.

Are you sucking up, or are you focused on building and understanding new relationships? Are you resentful and irritated that you have to have a bunch of smaller meetings before a big meeting, or do you recognize the power in being prepared, laying the groundwork, and giving your ideas the best chance of success? Do you view informal conversations as lobbying (with all the negative connotations this generally carries), or do you see them as doing important homework?

It's almost never about the activity itself, but rather the intention behind the activity and the interpretation and judgment we attach to both. Clearly, we tend to put more energy into something we see—and label—as positive and important than into those things we begrudge or don't see the point of doing.

Alternatively, if the negative connotations of office politics are so ingrained that you cannot change your mindset, try calling them something else. Tell yourself, "I am building strategic relationships with my stakeholders," or "I'm expanding my coalition of support."

What you call them doesn't matter. What does matter is that you see these things as valuable and important and put effort and energy into them.

Evaluate your style against your organization's political environment

Rather than spending your time and energy bemoaning or resenting the nature of organizations (which are inherently political), focus your time and energy on understanding what kind of political environment you're in.

Is your company minimally, moderately, highly, or pathologically politicized? To what degree does the political culture fit your (current) personal political style and what you want out of your life and career?

Kathleen Kelley Reardon, an expert on organizational politics, classifies political players into one of four types:[3]

- *The purist.* Do you dislike all thought of politics and simply want to get on with the job at hand?

- *The street fighter.* Do you believe the best way to get ahead is through the use of rough tactics, even at the expense of others?

- *The team player.* Do you believe in getting ahead by working well with others and participate in the politics that advance group goals?

- *The maneuverer.* Do you believe in getting ahead by playing the games of politics in a way that is skillful and unobtrusive to those who only take things at face value?

Of course, all of us can develop skills and change our approach if we really want to, but unless we make these changes, it's very unlikely that a purist will be happy or productive in a highly politicized environment or that a street fighter will be welcome in a minimally politicized environment.

Continuously work to strengthen your relationship currency

Focusing only on your relationship currency, or the credibility you build through your work, is very unlikely to get you the success you're aiming for—be it a bonus, promotion, or recognition from senior executives. However, investing time in your networks and building the connections that can speak for you and your work *will* get you those things. This investment in strategic relationships is not a distraction from your "real" job but in fact one of the most important aspects of it.

While it's clearly important to build relationships deliberately with people who can be your allies, don't make the mistake of neglecting to build relationships with people who have the potential to be your adversaries. Every additional adversary that you have lessens your political capital and your effectiveness.

You also need to understand where and how relationships are still being built, especially as the work environment becomes more virtual. WhatsApp chats? Virtual coffee meetings? Hour-long calls where there is no agenda other than to catch up with colleagues? If none of these are happening, perhaps you can start them, not only with people who are already in your network but also with those who you would like to have in your network.

Social media offers myriad opportunities to reach out to new connections outside of your organization. The value that this can offer your career is immense. A network that is as diverse and wide as possible has repeatedly been shown to be much more useful than a narrow, homogenous one.

Constantly improve your "political" savvy

To get to where you want to go, you need to be clear on where you are starting from. Understanding the concepts of political intelligence is one thing, but understanding how you stack up against them is another.

You will need to revisit and update your political strategy regularly as the context changes. You'll inevitably fail sometimes, but other times you'll succeed. Getting up and trying again is what matters. Winston Churchill said it well: "In war you can only be killed once. In politics you can be killed many times."

. . .

Remember that doing politics on your own terms, with a clear-eyed view of how to be effective without selling your soul or sacrificing your values, will benefit not only you but also those colleagues and stakeholders who are counting on you to do the best job you can. All of us play some form of politics, and getting better at the version that we want to play is critical to our career success and our personal well-being. Because it really is true—if you don't do politics, politics will do you.

QUICK RECAP

Office politics are a part of every organization, and you can't sit them out. If you typically seek to avoid office politics, you may need to reframe what they mean to you.

- Office politics are about relationship currency and influence capital—and the power these two things give you or don't give you.

- Focus on understanding your organization's political environment, how it suits your personal political style, and how you are going to be most effective in it.

- Investing in your networks and building connections who can speak for you and your work will get you the success you're aiming for.

Adapted from content posted on hbr.org, July 14, 2021.

Want to learn more about the essentials of office politics?
Listen to this episode of *Women at Work* from HBR:

12

Is Working with Your Romantic Partner a Good Match?

An interview with Sean Horan by Vasundhara Sawhney

From Harvey Specter and Donna Paulsen in *Suits* to Noh Ji-wook and Eun Bong-hee in *Suspicious Partner*, workplace romances are prevalent in popular media. IRL, too, crushing on a coworker is common: One SHRM survey found that half of U.S. workers have dated a colleague—mostly peers (70%) but also their supervisors (18%) and subordinates (21%).[1] In the United Kingdom, that number jumps to two-thirds of workers (66%).[2]

While some may find those metrics surprising, research shows that office romances are on the decline. The current climate around sexual harassment in the wake of the #MeToo movement has likely (and rightfully) played a factor, as has the rise of remote work. Still, when you consider that we spend most of our waking hours at our jobs (one-third of our lives), it seems inevitable that coworker crushes will arise from time to time. As humans, we have a basic need for intimacy and connection, but when we add attraction to this mix, we also add a layer of complexity.

How do office romances impact us, our work, and our relationship with peers?

I reached out to Professor Sean Horan, chair of the Department of Communication at Fairfield University, to learn more about what young professionals need to know. Sean and his research partner, Professor Rebecca Chory, have spent most of their careers trying to understand the implications of romantic relationships at work, both on our performance and on our team members.

Their research has specifically examined whether colleagues communicate with you differently if you're dating a coworker. Across three studies, they found that employees were more likely to lie to, distrust, and find peers dating their superiors less caring than peers dating other peers.[3] Though the studies initially focused on heterosexual relationships, Horan and Chory found similar results in a separate study examining gay and lesbian workplace romances.[4]

Our conversation highlighted some interesting (and alarming) aspects of how dating a coworker might influence your career. Here are some things you should consider before acting on a crush at work.

Vasundhara: *First things first: What's the spoiler alert?*

Sean: When you consider whether you want to engage in workplace romance, you should consider two things.

First, the vast majority of relationships, including those outside of a workplace romance, fail. Though there is a chance you may marry the person you're dating at work, the odds are not always in your favor. Think about what might happen if you break up but still work together.

Second, recognize that people will likely communicate with you differently and even view you differently. Can you live with that?

What is that difference? When your colleagues hear about your relationship, what changes?

Our research shows that employees are more likely to treat their peers differently when they are dating their own supervisor than dating someone at their own level, regardless of sexual orientation.

Colleagues are likely to feel that peers dating other organizational members, especially those who are senior to them, may have an unfair advantage or may receive preferential treatment over those employees who do not have a romantic partner at work. They might look at your accomplishments, assignments, duties, and rewards not as a sign of your competence but as an outcome of your relationship. We reasoned that the participants feared their peers would share negative information about them with their partners, especially if that partner happens to be a supervisor.

We also observed differences in perceptions of trustworthiness and caring in peer-superior versus peer-peer relationships. Employees reported that they perceived peers who dated supervisors as less trustworthy and caring—two major components of credibility— and noted feeling less close to those peers in comparison with the ones dating another colleague. When it came to trustworthiness, these perceptions were even more pronounced for female employees involved with a superior.

The pattern is clear: Workplace romance implications are more pronounced when people are in a peer-supervisor relationship.

So what should you do if you are dating a coworker or superior?

A few things, actually. First, learn your organization's dating policy. In our initial study on this topic, we found that while 56.5% of participants indicated their workplace had a rule banning romantic relationships among coworkers, 22.5% were "unsure" whether such a policy existed.[5]

Many organizations ban romantic relationships between people in reporting roles or insist on dating disclosures, so you need to know if what you're getting into is permissible. Reach out to your supervisor or human resources to understand who you might need to talk to if you're involved in an office relationship (or are planning to be in one).

Next, understand that your interpersonal relationships might change. Since perceptions have the potential to influence communication, think of how communication might change if you date a coworker or boss. The perception that a boss has a bias toward you or is giving you preferential treatment, for example, may lead your coworkers to "even the playing field" by withholding vital work-related information from you.

Our research found that employees reported being more likely to communicate deceptive or purposefully inaccurate information to those dating supervisors. This could be harmful to your job success in a workplace where accuracy of information is key and has implications on tasks, teams, and project success.

Then, think about whether you should make the relationship public. In an additional study I conducted with Professor Renee Cowan, we found that coworkers tended to react more positively when they learned of a workplace romance through a personal disclosure from the participant, compared with learning of it another way.[6] That said, if you want to be safe, whether your company has a policy or not, it would be wise to notify HR.

Lastly, if you're a manager dating a teammate (though this is prohibited in many organizations), think about how you'll deal with the impression you're making. Be clear, for example, on the grounds with which you award merit and opportunities to your partner as to avoid perceptions of unfairness. Better yet, consider having that person's annual performance and merit evaluations conducted by another person in a leadership role. You should also consider that there is a power dynamic happening here—you have more power than someone you are managing—and people may question your credibility, bias, and decisions.

I'm sensing a lot of caution.

In my study with Professor Cowan, we found that people primarily date at work because of perceived similarity, the amount of time spent together, the ease of opportunity, or to hook up. The reality is tougher to manage and should be managed with caution.

Beyond the judgments of your coworkers, think about whether you'll be able to work with this person without it affecting your job if you were to break up. Though everyone should break up in a respectful manner that maintains dignity and honors what you once shared, it doesn't always happen that way.

Given that you will see this person regularly at work and you both have a shared network, be sure to handle any breakup with dignity, respect, and care. You should both be able to leave this as adults with your heads held high. If that doesn't happen, speak with your HR to see if you can be transferred to another team and your reporting structure can be changed. In many cases, that is not a possibility, depending on the opportunities available at your company. Know that you may have to think about changing your company altogether if the breakup is messy. Ultimately, then, this represents another way dating at work can impact your career.

When exactly should you notify HR? Right away? As soon as it's official?

This could be tricky, too. Consider a situation where two employees go on three dates. After the first date, they notify HR. By the third, they realize it is not going anywhere. The problem here is that they already alerted HR to something being real and official when it didn't really exist long-term. Organizational policies actually force employees to face a relationship reality: *Is this really a relationship?*

Organizational policies, then, force those casually dating to have more serious conversations early on. Alert your HR once you have some clarity.

QUICK RECAP

Many of us spend most of our waking hours working, so it is inevitable that coworker crushes will arise from time to time.

Before starting an office romance, be aware how it might affect your work and your relationship with other colleagues:

- Consider what might happen if you break up or still work together.

- Whether you are dating a peer or supervisor matters—employees are more likely to distrust and lie to coworkers who are dating their superiors.

- Be aware of HR policies around dating in your organization. You may be required to disclose your status.

Adapted from "You're Crushing on a Coworker. Should You Go for It?" on hbr.org, September 23, 2021.

13

What to Do When You Become Your Friend's Boss

by Ben Laker, Charmi Patel, Ashish Malik, and Pawan Budhwar

How many hours will you spend with your coworkers over the course of your lifetime? If your job is a typical 9-to-5, that means you'll spend around eight hours a day, five days a week, for roughly 40 years, with the various people you work with. That equates to almost 90,000 hours total. So, a very long time.

Understandably, it would only make sense for some of these connections to blossom into something more personal, like friendships. And that's a good thing, because having friends at work has been proven to increase job satisfaction, performance, and even productivity.

But there is a flip side. Close friendships also have the potential to cause friction, especially for those of us who work in hierarchal environments. Once you are promoted into a leadership position, you will inevitably be required to make tough decisions and evaluate the people on your team fairly, whether or not those people are your friends. This presents a real challenge if you are a new manager transitioning from the role of "work friend" to the role of "boss." When one person in a friendship moves up, the dynamic changes from that of equals to one of meritocracy.

Navigating the boss-friend dynamic is even more difficult today than it was 15 years ago. Before the existence of iPhones and social media, people generally knew much less about each other's private lives, and they collaborated mostly during office house when colleagues were available in person. Today's technologies and social sharing have made us reachable around the clock. Social etiquette is vastly different: Workers are friends with their boss on Facebook, and they follow each other on Instagram and other social channels. It's common for workers to have their boss' cell number, meet their significant other, visit their manager's residence, and solicit advice from their manager on personal matters.

With the rise in work friendships—and everyone knowing perhaps a little *too* much about each other—our latest research sought to identify the most effective way to manage your relationship with friends at work when you become their boss. We surveyed 200 male and 200 female recently promoted, first-time managers across 17 countries between January and August 2020 and asked them the following questions (among others):

- How do you maintain relationships with colleagues you are friends with?

- What happened to your friendships when you were promoted?

- How have your friendships been affected since you started your new role?

- Which of your work friends are you connected to on social media? Which platforms?

- What has changed since taking up your new role?

- What do you miss about the times before you became a boss?

- How has your behavior changed since you were promoted?

- Do your friends influence your decision-making? If so, how?

- Who do you offload to in times of stress?

We found, rather worryingly, that more than 90% of these first-time managers have struggled to navigate the boundaries between being a boss and a friend, and more than 70% have lost friendships since becoming a manager. But this still didn't answer our question: How do you manage someone you used to be friends with, and do it well?

To explore this question further, we analyzed data from their responses and then conducted follow-up interviews. Our goal was to hear about their experiences in more detail and validate our findings. Through their responses, we identified five ways you can find the right balance between being a boss and a friend in the Information Age.

Acknowledge the power shift

Relationships are fluid, and the ones that last often involve open and clear communication. But for this to happen, the people involved must learn to renegotiate or rediscuss the parameters of their relationship as it changes over time. Interestingly, more than 80% of the first-time managers we surveyed did not address how their promotions changed the power dynamics with their former peers—and regretted waiting too long to do so. Many were not proactive about acknowledging the new meritocracy and assumed that any awkwardness that arose between themselves and their friends would disappear over time. But they were wrong. Many of their friendships suffered as a result.

Healthy relationships require a degree of honesty, often described as *radical candor*—the ability to address the problem at hand, even if the feedback is harsh (as long as it comes from a place of caring). If you are a new leader managing a friend, it's important to face the reality and acknowledge, sooner rather than later, that your relationship has changed. You can do this by taking time to speak candidly to your friend, explaining how you feel about your new dynamic and how you'd like to keep any awkwardness at bay. Denying your feelings of discomfort may cause you to come across as disingenuous. At the same time, you need to empathize with your friend's situation. You could say, "I'm a little uncomfortable, too, bringing this up, but I value our friendship, and I want to maintain the bond we have. Some parts of our relationship might change at work, and I think it's better we call them out now so we're on the same page."

Accept your new role

Your behavior as a new manager should be congruent with your new responsibilities. Many first-time managers we surveyed found this difficult to do and often fell back into "friend mode" with their closest colleagues, particularly those they were connected to on social media. This often occurred when they felt stressed or angry. Many resorted to gossiping carelessly about work challenges or sharing confidential information.

Once you are the boss, it's essential to be respectful and treat all your team members equally. Never gossip with your friend about colleagues. When you're a junior colleague chatting with peers, this kind of talk may be inevitable and may even make you feel closer. But as a leader, it's your job to fix friction between team members and find solutions—not to get caught up in the problems. If you set a bad example, you will lose credibility and trust. After all, who wants to be led by someone who spreads negativity and encourages drama?

When you need to vent, find a colleague you can confide in at your own level or a mentor with whom to share and offload. You must also take care to do so in a safe space—and never in the public realm of social media. Additionally, you can seek out a neutral party, like a coach, who has zero ties to your organization and your network.

Be consistent and fair with your team members

Another part of accepting your new role is being consistent in how you treat everyone on your team. This means that you cannot have favorites—and if you do, don't show it. If your team members suspect partiality, they may grow to resent you or the person you favor, and other toxic behavior could ensue.

For example, if you're heading out for lunch, extend the invitation to your whole team, not just those on your team you're most friendly with. In doing so, you may even discover new work-based friendships: In fact, more than 50% of our respondents reported developing new bonds with colleagues through this practice.

Don't let emotions get in the way of tough decisions

Being the boss means you have to accept that not everyone will like you, and that's OK. At the end of the day, the brutal truth is, you're required to make the tough decisions. That's why you're the boss. It's important for you to recognize that if you're friends with an employee, you may be blinded to their flaws or may not be able to place personal feelings aside so easily when you need to. This is why you have to be extra cautious about not letting your friendships influence your decisions, including raises, assignments, and layoffs.

Take layoffs, for example. This is probably the hardest leadership decision you'll ever face, and you should accept that letting go of employees (or firing a bad employee) is an unavoidable part of your job. You can't hold someone to a different set of standards just because you are friends—that's nepotism.

One way to treat everyone fairly is to put in place evaluation systems, such as objectives and key results, and use them for everyone equally so you're relying on objective, not subjective, data.

Manage how much you share on social media

We don't recommend befriending or following coworkers on social media, regardless of the platform. Your friends may use it to flaunt their bond with you, making their colleagues (your direct reports) jealous. For this reason, 10% of our respondents unfollowed and unfriended colleagues (and friends) after they were promoted. Many told us that doing so helped establish clearer boundaries and reduce the likelihood of oversharing. Others chose instead to tighten their privacy settings, allowing them to maintain a personal network in isolation from their work network.

Whichever strategy you adopt, our research suggests that outside of work, never share any information with your work friends that wouldn't be shared inside an office. In doing so, you could damage credibility and undermine all the preceding tips.

. . .

So remember, while workplace friendships have their benefits, they do have the potential to cause problems as your career paths diverge. Don't ignore the tough conversations. It's best to face the problem head-on as you transition from "work friend" to "boss."

QUICK RECAP

When one work friend is promoted to becoming another's boss, complicated power dynamics are introduced. It can be a struggle to navigate the boundaries between being a boss and a friend. To effectively manage this transition:

- **Acknowledge the power shift.** Have a conversation about the parameters of your friendships as they change.

- **Accept your new role.** Align your behavior with your new responsibilities.

- **Be consistent and fair with your team members.** Don't play favorites.

- **Don't let emotions get in the way of tough decisions.** Accept that not everyone will like you—and that's OK.

- **Manage how much you share on social media.** Consider tightening your privacy settings.

Adapted from content posted on hbr.org, September 24, 2020.

14

How to Give Negative Feedback to Your Peer

by Vasundhara Sawhney

Giving critical feedback is always going to be difficult. But giving it to a peer comes with its own set of challenges, especially if you have a good relationship. With an equal power dynamic between you, you have an even playing field. But if the feedback is delivered poorly, it can end up causing tension or result in the other person completely ignoring your words. Here's my advice:

Don't catch them off guard

For me, the one thing that has been a game changer is to never catch the other person off guard. Preparing the other person for your feedback allows you to explain your goodwill, set the tone for a positive conversation, and take them off the defensive.

Maybe you want to give your teammate feedback on their performance during a recent project. Maybe you want to ask them to respond to your emails more promptly. Or maybe they talked over other team members in a meeting, and you want to address it.

Whatever it is, reach out to them privately to set up a one-on-one meeting and explain what you want to discuss in a nonthreatening and open way. You might say something like, "Hey! I really enjoyed working with you on our last project, but I had some ideas around how we might be able to communicate better the next time around. Do you have time to meet for coffee this week and chat about it?"

Remember that feedback is not advice

The second thing to keep in mind is how you deliver your feedback. In this scenario, I'd make sure that your feedback doesn't come across as advice. Remember, this person is your peer. You don't want to sound condescending or unintentionally act like you're their boss. Advice is one-sided. Feedback is collaborative.

Keep it constructive

Lastly, make your feedback constructive. Focus on the problem, not the person. Let them know the positive outcome of changing their behavior. For example, if they took all the air space in a meeting, don't say, "You didn't let anyone else talk last meeting, and it was really rude." Instead, say: "I noticed you had some great ideas, but I think there were a few other people who also wanted to talk. Maybe next time, pause for a few seconds after sharing an idea to see if other people speak up. That's what I do in meetings, and it always leads to better brainstorming sessions. Some people just need more time to share than others."

QUICK RECAP

Giving negative feedback to a peer at work can be challenging, even if you have a good relationship. Keep three things in mind:

- **Don't catch them off guard.** Reach out to them privately to set up a one-on-one meeting and explain what you want to discuss in a nonthreatening and open way.

- **Remember that feedback is not advice.** Frame your feedback as a conversation you want to engage in.

- **Keep it constructive.** Focus on the behavior and its impact, not the person.

Adapted from "How to Give Negative Feedback to Your Peers, Boss, or Direct Reports" on hbr.org, April 11, 2023.

Want to learn more about how to work with a coworker you can't stand? Watch this video from HBR:

Networks, Mentors, and Sponsors

15

How to Strengthen Your Network When You're Just Starting Out

by Holly Raider

When you're just starting out, making new connections and strengthening your professional network are vital to getting to where you want to go. But the guidance you need, like how to thrive in a new role or pursue a promotion, can be difficult to find in your inner circle.

New employees tend to make professional connections based on proximity (colleagues they see the most) or commonalities (the colleagues most like themselves). But that's a mistake. When you network with colleagues like you or near you, you create an echo chamber that circulates only the same ideas about the same opportunities. That sameness benefits neither you nor your peers, especially when it comes to innovation and growth.

While it may be intimidating to leave the safety of your circle, you should. Strong, diverse networks help you stay on top of the latest trends in your industry, meet new collaborators, and gain access to opportunities or resources that can help you be more effective in your work. The best (yet often overlooked) way to build this kind of network is to focus on your lateral connections: peers who work in different areas of your company. Many early-career employees don't recognize how powerful these relationships can be.

Lateral connections give you a broader, more varied view of your organization, one that ultimately shapes the quality of your work and gives you access to breakthrough opportunities. Let's say you are a sales associate who has limited interactions with a coordinator on the product development team. Taking the initiative to form a relationship with that person could expose you to the innovations they are working on, allowing you to gain a deeper understanding of each product and equipping you with the personal stories behind their development. Those insights and stories will enable you to be far more effective in making a sale. Meanwhile, the product coordinator will learn from you exactly how a customer thinks when deciding whether to buy the product, allowing your colleague to make smarter suggestions fueled by customer insights during brainstorming meetings.

This is just one example of how mutually beneficial these cross-departmental relationships can be. Strengthening your interdepartmental network can also give you access to opportunities that may be brewing in other parts of your company before they become public.

So how exactly can you start?

Look for people you can learn from

During companywide or cross-departmental meetings, pay attention and make note of the people and projects you find most interesting. It's best to be strategic about this—don't reach out only to those who seem like they'd make a good friend; reach out to those whose work has some intersection with your own. If you're an editor, think about connecting with the graphic designers whose work complements your writing. If you're in finance, consider reaching out to your peers in sourcing and discuss with them how the company manages currency fluctuations or transportation costs.

Meet up

A helpful way to build lateral connections is by attending or planning events with people who are not on your team. If you work in person, message a couple of peers in other departments with whom you'd like to connect and ask if they'd like to grab a quick lunch. If you're working remotely, virtual group happy hours or coffee breaks are good options. Conversations that occur during these meetings are often informal and free-flowing. Remember, your goal should be building strong relationships, not just exchanging notes about work. That starts with getting to know people.

Be sure to follow up with those you most want to keep up with. You might send them a quick email the next day, saying, "Hi! I'm [ ] and I joined [ ] days ago." Then state something personal to make the connection, like, "I heard during the virtual happy hour that you're learning Spanish on Duolingo. I was excited to hear that as I'm interested in studying a second language, too." Finally, make a small request: "Would you like to meet for coffee and chat a bit more sometime?"

People usually enjoy talking about their experiences, so if your questions are respectful and specific, it's rare that they will turn you down. This is a great way to start things off. You will inspire each other and, better yet, help each other solve problems through sharing your diverse experiences and expertise.

Create or join online chat groups

If you're working remotely, take advantage of apps like Slack. Find out if there are existing chat groups you could join. If not, you could take the lead on setting up channels for specific topics (and they don't have to be about work!). Think travel, tech, cooking, gardening, film, or a word-of-the-day group. Begin by asking your colleagues what topics they are most interested in discussing, then bring together the group virtually.

For starters, you and the other people in the group will have one thing in common: the reason you joined it. Generate active participation by asking a colleague or two to jump-start the chat. Others will follow suit organically.

Say yes more often

Another excellent strategy for building lateral connections is to embrace assignments that involve collaboration with new counterparts in the organizations. If your company has volunteer opportunities, such as the sustainability committee, social planning committee, or DEI committees, volunteer. These are often cross-departmental opportunities and are a valuable way to get to know people you'd normally not work with. You can learn about these opportunities at your company's intranet, via e-newsletters, and by asking your supervisor or HR representative.

Many companies have social opportunities as well. One of my mentees, an internal sales representative, found out about her company's softball team by talking with her peers in another department. Through this, she has friendships with peers she would not otherwise have met. Also check out your company's learning and development website. It will have information on short courses, which are a terrific way to build your skills and meet new people.

Show curiosity to transform a connection into a relationship

Once you have made an initial connection, you can build toward a strong relationship that makes the most of your complementary skills and experiences. Start with showing your interest in understanding others' work by asking specific questions, and even asking for advice that would be easy for them to give. For example, if a colleague in human resources gives a presentation that intrigues you, let them know and see if they could spare 20 to 30 minutes helping you prepare for a presentation you are developing. By asking for help, you will receive valuable assistance and strengthen your connection along the way. As Ben

Franklin wrote in his autobiography, "He that has once done you a kindness will be more ready to do you another, than he whom you yourself have obliged." Start there, but be sure to provide reciprocity—a one-sided connection is not a pathway to a strong relationship.

. . .

These strategies are straightforward, but too often are overlooked and undervalued. Making lateral connections is important for not just strengthening your network but also leading you to new opportunities. They can help you be more effective in your work and spark great ideas by bridging the different worlds of knowledge you will have available through your network—not to mention, they are some of the easiest to achieve.

QUICK RECAP

Building a strong, diverse lateral network will help you stay on top of industry trends, meet new collaborators, and gain access to opportunities or resources that can help you be more effective.

- **Look for people you can learn from.** Make note of the people and projects you find most interesting.

- **Meet up.** Attend or plan events with people who are not on your team.

- **Create or join online chat groups.** They don't have to be about work.

- **Say yes more often.** Embrace assignments that involve collaboration with new counterparts.

- **Show curiosity to transform a connection into a relationship.** Ask them for help—and provide it to them.

Adapted from content posted on hbr.org, November 13, 2020.

Want to learn more about how to build your network from scratch?
Listen to this episode of *New Here* from HBR:

16

When It Comes to Promotions, It's About Who Knows You

by Anand Tamboli

During my days at LG Electronics, January was the month of promotions. The office filled with whispers of who would be next to advance. We all had our theories. We were also almost always wrong.

I remember one particular afternoon, when a colleague of mine, Arun, was passed up for a promotion, leaving the entire office confused. He was an excellent engineer with strong leadership skills—someone we would have bet money on. We all thought he deserved it.

"Arun has so many years of experience," I said to my manager, Mr. Kim. "He's great at what he does. Why didn't he get the promotion?"

"Arun is an excellent engineer, no doubt," Mr. Kim said. "But he isn't ready to be a manager yet." Seeing my surprised expression, he added, "Arun needs to develop stronger relationships with people across the organization. That kind of collaboration is key for the manager role."

The words stuck with me.

After three and a half years at LG, I moved on to HSBC as a project manager. I worked relentlessly to ensure I fulfilled the needs of the job and was intentional about building strong connections with people across the organization. When performance reviews rolled around, I was confident about my chances for advancement. But again, I was surprised by my manager's response.

"Look," my boss, Peter, said, "I'm not questioning your skill set. But to be considered seriously for a more senior role, you need to gain the support of more people in the company—influential people who can speak to your work and advocate for you when you're not in the room. My voice alone isn't enough. You need a network of champions!"

Something clicked. There it was—the secret ingredient so many of us are missing when we lose out on opportunities. Most of us spend our time learning a craft, networking with our peers, and avoiding big mistakes. This is useful in the earliest days of our careers, but as we grow, so do the criteria for advancement. The higher we climb, the more we need people in senior roles to back us. In a perfect world, talent and leadership competency alone would be enough. But unfortunately, that's not always how it works, and until things change, this knowledge is power.

How to Make Yourself Known

Over the years, I've developed a tool to help people at all levels take advantage of this information: a career progression ladder outlining what you should prioritize in the first five to seven years of your career to fast-track your advancement (see figure 16-1).

During your first year in the workforce, *what you know* is the most important. In the earliest days of a new job, you spend much of your time developing the competencies and base-level knowledge essential to succeeding in your role. Those skills often determine your eligibility for advancement.

A few years in, when you've gained expertise in your function or domain, *who you know* becomes just as important as your

FIGURE 16-1

A career progression ladder

Know which stages to prioritize in the first five to seven years of your career.

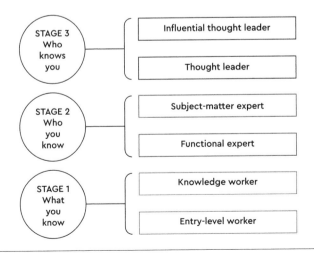

skill set—especially if you wish to move up into a management role. This stage is all about expanding your professional network. Your relationships with people at different levels and on different teams throughout your company will help you understand how the organization functions at large, how the various departments work together, and how the goals of the team you seek to lead fit into the bigger picture.

The tipping point comes after you've gained some experience as a people manager and are well-rounded in your subject matter or field. At this point, you may feel that you're ready to lead a larger team or take on a senior-level role. This is where *who knows you* matters.

But you cannot begin finding your champions—influential people who will rally for you and put their trust in you—when you need them. Your champions are either the decision-makers themselves (the people who decide who gets promoted) or powerful people who the decision makers will listen to.

This is perhaps the most challenging stage of your career: when you're moving from being a new leader to a slightly more seasoned leader. Connecting with influential people throughout your organization presents unique challenges that are harder to navigate than what was required of you in the years prior. So how exactly do you go about it?

In my experience, you need to focus on three things: positioning, publishing, and collaborating.

Positioning

To build trust and reliability with influential people, you need to establish yourself as someone who is dependable. This means that all your actions, behaviors, and words need to be consistent and predictable. You need to make an intentional effort to "position" yourself the way you want others to see you as a person and professional.

For example, let's take a closer look at the case of Arun, my colleague at LG Electronics. Our manager, Mr. Kim, didn't perceive him as a leader. He wasn't sure if Arun had the collaboration skills required to be a great people manager. Why? Because Mr. Kim couldn't predict how Arun would respond to challenging situations, teach his direct reports new skills, or work with colleagues across departments to accomplish goals.

Arun was consistent in demonstrating his technical abilities, but he never exemplified his leadership chops. He spoke often about the nitty-gritty steps required to successfully complete his projects and spoke little about the ways he was working with his team members to solve problems or provide them with guidance.

Likewise, when I put in for a promotion, my manager couldn't predict if I would align with other senior leaders in the company. At the time, I had made little effort to connect with and understand the work happening in other departments and how that work connected back to my own role. Had I done so publicly—had I gained the trust of those other leaders and discussed my learnings with Peter—he may have perceived me as leadership material.

Publishing

Other people don't know what's going on in your head: your thoughts, ideas, opinions, passions, and visions for the future. If you want these things to be known, you need to make them visible. You need to publish.

To start, do a self-audit. Ask yourself: "Am I voicing my views aloud and enough? Do I speak up when it matters? What can I create to make myself and my presence known?"

There are several ways to go about this. You can write and share your ideas on social media platforms like LinkedIn or Twitter, author articles and pitch them to media outlets, or even create videos to post on TikTok, Instagram, or YouTube. In this context, "publishing" can also mean using your voice to share ideas. This could involve signing up for public speaking engagements or simply raising your hand more in meetings. Choose whatever works for you, your level of comfortability, and your intended audience.

Let's assume that your team has spearheaded a project you're especially proud of. Consider posting your thoughts about the work on a platform like LinkedIn or authoring a short thought piece about the impact you made and why it's important. While this may seem unrelated to your actual job, sharing your published work is a great way to draw the attention of power players within your organization. It shows that you're passionate and has the potential to strengthen your authority on the topic at hand, positively influencing how others perceive you. Thought leaders in various industries take this approach to get their ideas out into the world and establish themselves as changemakers in their fields.

Collaborating

Networking is great for making new connections, but collaborating with people across your organization is a better way to build meaningful and long-lasting relationships. When people with different expertise come together to achieve a common goal, learning opportunities flourish. Each person is given a chance to contribute their unique skill set and perspective, and through this teamwork, bonds are built. When we teach other people, or vice versa, growth takes place—and we remember the people who help us grow because we see their value.

As a rising leader, you should attempt to collaborate with your senior colleagues whenever the chance arises. If you can show them your value, they will support you in future endeavors and may even become your champions or ambassadors down the line.

The hard part is seeking out these collaboration opportunities. It can be a daunting task if you work at an organization in which cross-functional teamwork is not super accessible or common. If this is the case, reach out to your manager and ask for their help. You could say, "I'm interested in learning more about the work that takes place in X department. I noticed they have a project coming up—would it be OK if I shadowed a few of their meetings? I wonder if my perspective would be valuable. Since our teams are working toward a common goal, I could share what we've learned through our own work."

In all cases, think about what you can uniquely offer through a collaboration. For instance, as a Gen Zer, could your perspective be interesting to the marketing team on their new campaign? As a tech guru, could your experience analyzing data be valuable to the content team? What can you offer the leaders in other departments to help them reach their goals?

· · ·

Now let's go back to my story. When Peter told me to double down, I did exactly that. I became clearer about my positioning, elevated my voice and ideas through publication, and sought out more ways to collaborate with leaders throughout the company. With my fierce efforts (and some luck), I secured the promotion. I still remember and follow Peter's advice today. I hope it will help you on your journey, too.

QUICK RECAP

During your first year in the workforce, *what you know* is the most important. A few years in, when you've gained expertise, *who you know* becomes just as important. Later, when you're ready to lead, *who knows you* matters. How do you go about making this leap?

- **Positioning.** To build trust and reliability with influential people, establish yourself as someone who is dependable.

- **Publishing.** Make your thoughts, ideas, opinions, passions, and visions for the future visible and known.

- **Collaborating.** Work with senior colleagues whenever the chance arises. When you show them your value, they will support you in future endeavors.

Adapted from "When It Comes to Promotions, It's About Who Knows You . . . Not Who You Know" on hbr.org, September 7, 2022.

17

Networking Skills for Professionals from Underrepresented Backgrounds

by AiLun Ku and Ray Reyes

Professionals from historically underrepresented backgrounds (including BIPOC professionals, first-generation college graduates and white-collar workers, and those from low-income households) are often told by well-meaning advisers to "network for opportunities" without further guidance. But without understanding how to navigate the hidden rules of engagement—the "cheat codes" that are passed down generationally among predominantly represented groups—many of these professionals are unable to gain entry to the majority white and privileged networks that control access to quality jobs, projects, and resources. For underrepresented professionals, networking can feel like negotiating a labyrinth blindfolded. Many believe they need to present a fabricated and inauthentic version of themselves to have a better chance of getting past a heavily guarded gate into the land of career opportunities.

We believe that there is a better way for underrepresented professionals to network—a way that allows them to garner support and access and move their careers forward while remaining true to themselves. In our work as executives at the Opportunity Network, a nonprofit devoted to supporting students from underrepresented backgrounds through college and into thriving careers, we have seen thousands of individuals grow their professional networks and use them successfully to advance at work.

If you are a member of an underrepresented group, especially if you are early in your career, this is a paradoxical moment. Despite the rhetorical support that most workplaces now profess for greater diversity, equity, and inclusion, reality hasn't caught up. The benefits that professional networks grant still skew away from those faced with systemic barriers. But that doesn't mean you can't network successfully and amass social currency in the workplace. To build a wide and diverse professional community that will help you move up—and ultimately help you bring up others along with you—you must understand and navigate three lingering networking paradoxes that affect underrepresented individuals. Let's explore each in turn.

The "Authentic Self" Paradox

The first paradox is the tension between code-switching and authenticity. Cornell professor Courtney McCluney and her coauthors describe *code-switching* as behavior in which one changes their "style of speech, appearance, behavior, and expression in ways that will optimize the comfort of others in exchange for fair treatment, quality service, and employment opportunities." Being falsely perceived as "unprofessional" due to unconscious bias or divergence from dominant norms has real consequences. It can limit access to opportunities, information, and resources and ultimately derail career advancement. In response, professionals from historically underrepresented groups, particularly BIPOC professionals, often choose to weave code-switching into their workday. They may adjust their self-presentation by mirroring the norms, behaviors, and attributes of peers from dominant groups.

In the networking context, the drive to code-switch is heightened. Ongoing concern about meeting unknown—and possibly biased—people in situations that are layered with subtext and unspoken rules discourages underrepresented professionals from entering networking spaces as their authentic selves. However, code-switching is merely a tool for survival, not the answer. Beyond placing the undue burden of conformity and assimilation on people from historically underrepresented groups, code-switching is the erasure of one's identity, an unsustainable sacrifice. Code-switching ensures safe and vacuous interaction, but it prevents you from making real connections and decays your overall well-being in the long run. How can you extend yourself to others when it isn't safe to show up as yourself? How can you be your best when you can't be you?

To manage this tension, we encourage you to reveal your authentic self gradually. The gradual-reveal approach doesn't ask you to contort your identity to fit another mold. Instead, it allows you to remain true to yourself while asserting your agency in which parts of yourself you want to share and when.

First, understand that how much to disclose at work is a balancing act for everyone. While your CEO probably feels safe showing up at work, they aren't going to share all the details from their Saturday night, and you shouldn't either. Your colleagues are not your friends and family, and total disclosure is not your goal. Set and maintain professional boundaries while observing the extent to which racially based comparisons, however subtle, drive social interactions in your workplace. Next, put out a feeler—share as much of your authentic self as you feel comfortable and safe doing with a single colleague or a small group. Pay attention to how your colleague responds, and match yourself to the intensity and depth of the exchange. If the sharing is reciprocated and mutually beneficial, you may feel safe to reveal more. The gradual-reveal approach can be challenging to implement in networking settings where you'll be meeting people who are truly unknown to you. Whenever possible, lean on a trusted connection from your growing network to gather information in advance. If you do end up in a conversation in which a gradual reveal isn't going well, be prepared to politely move to a neutral topic and then bring the exchange to an end; this person isn't likely to be a supporter, and you don't need to waste your time with them.

The "Gatekeeper" Paradox

The second paradox is that networks can be both stubborn gatekeepers and transformative door openers. The race to hire qualified, diverse talent is always on, and few organizations are keeping up. This narrow pipeline is chiefly the result of gated networks' tendency to value exclusivity and selectivity over diversity and expansiveness. This approach might have worked when firms were looking for cookie-cutter candidates from a short list of schools or a small circle of contacts, but these old ways simply do not achieve the new results that organizations are looking for.

The reductive truism "It's who you know" serves an outdated version of professional networks that keep the gates shut. These networks concentrate power among those who know about jobs, decide who else gets to know about jobs, who gets hired, who gets mentored, and who gets promoted. These most in-the-know networkers end up wielding outsize influence. Absent deliberate intervention, this power imbalance sustains homogeneous networks and perpetuates a homogeneous workforce.

However, the widespread awakening to the need for a more diverse workforce, technological advances, as well as "the Great Resignation" have flipped the script. With the wide adoption of social media, everyone has the tools to be a transformative door opener instead of a stubborn gatekeeper. Knowing this, we encourage underrepresented professionals to adopt an asset-based mindset: Recognize that you undeniably and intrinsically bring something valuable to the table. You have a reserve of tacit critical-thinking and problem-solving skills gained through your lived experience; you are fluently bilingual and can competently navigate between cultures with care and confidence because you do it daily. This self-awareness will enable you to network confidently and present yourself as the missing piece to employers' hiring puzzle. With an asset-based mindset, you shift the "it's who you know approach from *getting past the gatekeeper* who knows about the job to *meeting the door opener* whose network is expansive enough to identify, attract, and recruit qualified

talent (like you) from a candidate pool that has been historically untapped and underrepresented.

The "Proximity" Paradox

The final paradox requires professionals from underrepresented
backgrounds to grow their close-knit professional circles into
more expansive networks in order to increase their social proximity to networks of power and influence. Social proximity
boosts social capital. And while it may seem like a contradiction,
particularly if you are new in your career, social capital is intrinsically embedded in relationships in every direction, so we
encourage you to invest time in building a network that is broad
and deep—and attend to it. Networks are living structures that
require nurturing and pruning.

Of course, networking upward will help you gain access to
mentors and sponsors, relationships that are critical to your long-
term career success. But don't neglect networking laterally with
peer and near-peer groups. Forming a network of peers boosts
your self-confidence and provides the support you need to over-
come the hurdle of soliciting new connections beyond familiar
circles. Networking with midcareer professionals and near-
peers also can help demystify the hidden rules of work that lie
just ahead.

Finally, don't neglect reaching out to those coming up after
you. A 360-degree network-building approach gives you connections and resources to meet varying needs. It also develops the
habit of giving career support to others while creating the opportunity to receive it.

With an expansive network, you can build a personal board of directors, a group of trustworthy people ready to offer critical and encouraging feedback to you. This group could include a mentor, a personal friend, someone from whom you seek counsel, someone who is well informed in your workplace or industry, and someone who can connect you to opportunities. Among your board, you should feel safe and comfortable enough to honestly grapple with challenges, receive candid and constructive feedback, be supported with unconditional regard, and be able to show up as your authentic self.

. . .

Code-switching, barriers to entry, and navigating power dynamics all take their toll. Networking can be tiring for anyone; to underrepresented individuals, it can be downright exhausting. But the first step to overcoming these challenges is being aware of the three paradoxes and managing them proactively. This must be reinforced by personal wellness and self-care practices—and leaning on the support of your growing network—to remain balanced when obstacles inevitably arise.

We hope that you and every underrepresented professional have the chance to operate from a safe space with access to soft landings as you help close the opportunity gap by building networks and exchanging social capital. Expansive networks traverse ethnicity, language, geography, age, physical ability, gender identity (pay attention to people's pronouns), sexual orientation, social status, educational and training experience, and life experience. The more diverse your professional networks, the greater your access to information and connections and the sooner you will be in a place of abundant social capital and able to raise others up along with you.

QUICK RECAP

The unfortunate reality is that more-privileged groups continue to control access to the majority of jobs and career opportunities. Individuals from underrepresented communities should learn to navigate three paradoxes as they grow their networks:

- **The "authentic self" paradox.** Start by reaching out to just one person on your team, or in your office, for an informal, one-on-one conversation to see if they can be your ally.

- **The "gatekeeper" paradox.** Adopt an asset-based mindset and recognize that the things that make you different give you distinct skills and experience.

- **The "proximity" paradox.** Network at all levels—people in senior positions, peers, and those junior to you.

Adapted from *HBR Guide to Smarter Networking* (product #10555E), Harvard Business Review Press, 2022.

18

What's the Difference Between a Mentor and a Sponsor?

by Janice Omadeke

Mentorship and sponsorship are powerful tools for personal success and building stronger workforces. Although they are related to one another and share some similarities, they are not, as most people sometimes assume, the same thing. In reality, sponsorship can grow from a productive mentor-mentee relationship.

What is mentorship?

In a work setting, *mentorship* is a relationship between someone sharing knowledge and providing guidance (the mentor) and someone learning from that person's experience and example (the mentee).

Most of the time, the mentor is older and the mentee is younger—perhaps new to the workforce—but mentorship can exist and thrive in any situation where a new employee is learning from a more experienced one. Contrary to what you might assume, a mentor does not have to be somebody in management. In fact, people who aren't in management can derive great satisfaction and sense of contribution from mentoring someone else.

Mentorship can start with something as simple as an informational coffee and can take various forms from there. It could just be a onetime meeting, but the most valuable mentorships grow over time as evolving peer-to-peer relationships. While mentorship is usually between just two people, group mentorship is an approach that businesses sometimes take as well. It can occur in person or online.

What is sponsorship?

The image of sponsorship that probably first comes to mind is that of a professional athlete being boosted by a business, like a top soccer player receiving a lot of their gear from a company that makes it. In turn, they promote that company's brand by wearing and using the products.

That's not the kind of sponsorship we're talking about in this context. Here, *sponsorship* stems from a strong and successful mentorship.

Think of it as phase two of mentorship. Once the mentor and mentee have worked together for a while, usually at least a few months, the mentor may see evidence of growth and self-accountability in the mentee. At that point, the mentor can become an actual advocate for their mentee. In this capacity, the mentor is now a sponsor and the mentee is a protégé.

Now the sponsor is doing more than just sharing experience and knowledge. Because they have come to feel personally invested in the advancement of the protégé, the sponsor expands that person's visibility within the organization, models self-advancing behavior, and directly involves the protégé in experiences that will provide opportunities for career advancement. For instance, a sponsor may put their protégé's name on the table for a promotion, or have the power to advocate for their work when they are not in the room (or invited to the "important" meeting themselves).

The sponsor is putting their reputation and professional branding behind the protégé, meaning there's typically more risk to being a sponsor. This is why sponsorship is more likely to develop from an effective mentorship. In short, the mentorship develops the trust and confidence requisite for sponsorship to occur.

Why do you need both?

One takeaway so far is that mentorship is a critical step toward establishing a sponsorship. While not all mentorships will develop into sponsorships, that doesn't mean mentorship doesn't have other benefits. Here are some of them:

- People learn more about each other, which strengthens the workforce overall, as coworkers begin to see each other as unique individuals and not just fellow workers who exist to check off a list of tasks to complete.

- The mentee has extra support in reaching their goals. They can work together with their mentor in a structured setting to do so.

- Mentees attain the professional skills they will need to advance in their careers.

- Mentorship affords mentees an opportunity to form meaningful relationships and feel included as a valuable part of a company and its culture. This is especially the case with hybrid and remote workers now making up a larger share of the workforce and with younger workers who may have no prior experience as a part of it.

- Mentors can find fulfillment in passing on knowledge and having a leadership role even if their positions are not in management.

Mentorship, then, is valuable purely for its own sake.

Sponsorship, as we've seen, starts with mentorship and builds on it. Mentorship provides the concrete details and other experiences that the sponsor can use to advocate for their protégé.

. . .

Working at a company with a mentorship program or seeking out a mentor at work, then, is a proven way to invest in your growth as an employee just entering the workforce or even simply a new role. If you invest enough time and effort into the relationship, you may just end up with a sponsor as well, and what could be better than both?

QUICK RECAP

Mentorship and sponsorship are powerful tools for personal success and building stronger workforces. Although they are related to one another and share some similarities, they are not, as people sometimes assume, the same thing.

- **Mentorship** involves a mentor sharing knowledge and providing guidance with a mentee, who is learning from the mentor's experience and example.

- **Sponsorship** involves a sponsor increasing a protégé's visibility within the organization, modeling self-advancing behavior, and directly involving the protégé in experiences that will provide opportunities for career advancement.

Adapted from content posted on hbr.org, October 20, 2021.

Want to learn more about how sponsorship can benefit your career?
Listen to this episode of *Women at Work* from HBR:

What's the Right Way to Find a Mentor?

by Janet T. Phan

In the summer of 2004, I was 18 years old, preparing for my first year of college and looking for ways to fund my education. I was working double shifts at KFC and late nights at Hollywood Video, yet one day, I found myself at a gas station without enough money to fill up my tank.

I made a promise to myself to do whatever it would take never to be in this situation again: one where I was living from paycheck to paycheck, working multiple jobs, and couch surfing to save money on rent. Working harder—in my case, 12-hour days—wasn't getting me anywhere, but I knew that working smarter could. As the child of refugee parents from Vietnam, I didn't have anyone at home who understood how to navigate the American school system or workforce. I knew I needed help, someone to guide me.

A good mentor can make a huge imprint on your life, and it is thanks to not one, but many, that I was able to grow from that woman stuck at the gas station into who I am now. I turned to my former high school teacher, a person I could trust, who advocated for my education and gave me advice that prepared me to succeed in college. Once I graduated, I started an IT internship where I met a mentor who, six years later, helped me land a job in tech. Today, I'm a global technology program manager for one of the world's largest firms and founder of Thriving Elements, a nonprofit mentoring program for underserved, underrepresented girls around the globe.

My work has taught me some valuable lessons, but perhaps the most important is that no matter what stage you're at, it's worth learning how to make an ask, nurture, and maintain these kinds of relationships. Fostered correctly, they can put you in the driver's seat of your career, empower you to explore options that were previously unimaginable, give you access to untapped opportunities, and teach you how to navigate the challenges you never saw coming.

Here are a few tips on how you can find mentors and maintain and nurture those relationships.

Ask for that first meeting

Seventy-six percent of people say that mentors are important, but only 37% actually have one.[1] Why the gap? In my experience, it's because most people are afraid to ask for that initial meeting. The fear of rejection is real, and it's even more amplified during this pandemic.

Reaching out to someone you admire but whom you may not know so well—especially if that person is more senior than you—is intimidating.

To take some pressure off yourself and ease the fear, remind yourself that the people you admire have likely had various mentors throughout their lives who have helped them get to where they are today and would jump at the opportunity to help others in the same way. If you want to connect with them, start with a simple ask: a quick 15- to 30-minute meeting.

The best way to reach out is usually to send a short email. Share one or two things you admire about their work, then tell them a little about yourself, why you're reaching out, and what you would like to learn from them. Then wrap it up with your ask:

> Dear X,
>
> I've been reading about the work you're doing with Y. I'm interested in building my career in technology, and I'd love to hear how you rose from a systems analyst to a technical product manager in five years. Would it be possible for us to have a quick video chat sometime within the next couple of weeks?

A first meeting over coffee, or a short video call, is low commitment for your target mentor and will give you an opportunity to better understand them, gauge your chemistry, and see if they'd be the right fit for you.

Nurture the relationship

The number one recommendation I've heard from both the mentors and the mentees I've worked with over the years is: Take the time to really connect with the other person.

Get to know them. Think of your first coffee meeting or virtual call as an opportunity for casual conversation. Remember that you're both still feeling each other out, so don't just focus the discussion on work. Ask your potential mentor what they like to do on the weekends, what books they like to read, or what hobbies they're interested in. Most people will be thrilled to take a break from their hectic workdays and connect on a personal level. This kind of conversation also gives you both a chance to see if you have anything in common and whether or not you enjoy each other's company.

Toward the middle of the first meeting, it's appropriate to bring up career questions you have for them and talk about the areas in which you'd like to grow. As you wrap up, summarize the advice they've provided to show that you value their input. For instance, you might say, "It sounds like attending networking events really helped you advance your career. I'll look into some virtual meetups that I can use to connect with other people in my field. Thanks for that suggestion."

Send a thank-you note. After your meeting, follow up with a thank-you email sometime within the same week. In your message, share a few key things you learned during the conversation, and let them know you'd like to follow up in a few weeks:

> Dear X,
>
> I loved learning about your hike in Vietnam and all the wonderful food you tried along the way. I think I might go to the Vietnamese restaurant nearby and give the cuisine a try. I was also surprised to hear that

you taught yourself how to code through online courses. That is so inspiring! If it's OK with you, I'll touch base in a few weeks.

Most people in a position to mentor are busy, so don't be alarmed if it takes them a few days to respond.

Follow up. Three to five weeks after sending the thank you message, follow up to let your potential mentor know what you did based on your discussions in that first meeting (did you read the book they recommended or watch a TED Talk they seemed to have loved?). Then ask if they would be willing to meet up again within the next couple of weeks. I don't recommend sending an agenda. Rather, try to keep your tone and suggestions casual. In my experience, good leaders and mentors appreciate a more informal setting. The point is to create an atmosphere that's enjoyable for both of you—not schedule yet another work meeting. That said, it can be helpful to note down things that you'd like to discuss and share them in your email when reaching out:

Dear X,

I finally got down to reading that book and I have to say, I can't believe I didn't read it sooner. What a great story of grit and determination. Thank you for recommending it.

I was planning to take a course in creative writing from Y institute. Are you familiar with it? Maybe we can discuss during our next catch-up? I know you're

very busy, but let me know if you'd have time to
meet up in the next couple of weeks. I'd really
appreciate it.

Usually after three or four meetings, you'll have a good sense of whether you'd like the person to be your mentor, at which point you can say something like, "These meetings have been very helpful to me; it's almost like you're my mentor!" Then pause and see their reaction.

If they reciprocate with a yes, that's good news for you. If they smile but don't respond directly, that's OK too. It's likely because they don't want to formally commit to mentorship right now. But don't be discouraged. As long as they're making time to meet with you and you're getting the guidance you need, there's really no need for a label.

Maintain the relationship

When you ask someone to be your mentor, you are also asking them to invest their time in you. Show them that their time is being well used by demonstrating a return on their investment.

Keep them updated. As a mentor myself, I can say there's nothing more rewarding than seeing that the time I've invested in a mentee was valuable and helped them advance toward their goals. But it's a mentee's job to help the mentor see just how they've done so. Remember that first follow-up email you sent? Make that a regular thing. Use the time between your catch-ups to take action on the goals you set with your mentor. Send them updates (a simple text or an email) telling them how their guidance is playing an important role in your career and personal development. But be sure not to spam them. About once every month or two is good during the first year, and as time progresses and you've established a good mentoring relationship, pinging your mentor even once a quarter is OK. The goal is to keep in touch and to keep them informed about how your career is progressing.

Offer to help. As with any relationship, mentoring relationships are a two-way street. What you're giving back to your mentor is really your progress, but there's also no harm in checking in with your mentor during your meetings to see if you can help them in any way. Maybe they're working on a presentation and could use an outside perspective, or perhaps you know someone they were looking to connect with.

Express gratitude. Write a thank-you note after each meeting. While it doesn't need to be as extensive as your first note, a quick "Thanks again for your time, was great to catch up!" will show them that you appreciate the time and guidance they are giving to you.

· · ·

Mentorship can be life-changing. I'm proof of that. Staying in the driver's seat and being proactive will make your relationship with your mentor a successful one. Use these principles to guide you toward a future you've imagined for yourself.

QUICK RECAP

A mentor can empower you in ways that were previously unimaginable. Use these principles to develop and maintain a strong mentoring relationship, no matter where you are in your career.

- **Ask for the first meeting.** A coffee or video call is low commitment for your target mentor and will give you an opportunity to assess fit.

- **Nurture the relationship.** Take the time to really connect with the other person and don't focus only on work. Send a thank-you note to show your gratitude.

- **Maintain the relationship.** Keep them updated on your progress, offer to help, and show you appreciate the time and guidance they are giving to you.

Adapted from content posted on hbr.org, March 10, 2021.

Want to learn more about finding a mentor who can accelerate your career? Watch this video from HBR:

Build a Circle of Advisers

by Mimi Aboubaker

Everyone could benefit from having a circle of advisers—an informal group of people you trust, whose knowledge and perspectives you can call on when working through decisions—to supercharge your professional (and personal) trajectory.

The term *mentor* is often anchored to this kind of relationship, but I find it limiting. For many, the "shoulds" and "shouldn'ts" attached to mentorship are stressful and can become a deterrent to pursuing much-needed support. Instead, I'd recommend swapping the term for *adviser* and referring back to your high school days for a more approachable model.

In high school, students are often given the opportunity to develop informal advising or support relationships with a mix of people. You may have had this experience. These relationships typically form organically and can include academic advisers, athletic coaches, family, neighbors or community members, and even peers and near-peers. Together, these people make up a support network.

The professional world is similar. Your circle of advisers includes people with varying specialties. You have different levels of connection with each of them, and your relationships have the potential to strengthen over time. There are, however, a few important distinctions that can make finding advisers in your early career more challenging than it was in your teens:

- *Your priorities.* During your adolescence, classes, college, and fitting in socially were likely top of mind. As a young professional, your priorities have probably shifted to career growth, finding the right job or organization, and fitting in culturally at your firm (for example, interpersonal dynamics, office politics, and so on).

- *Your level of initiative.* For many of us, support networks were built into our high school or college experiences, especially if they included our family members, friends, or instructors. In the professional world, you have to proactively recruit supporters.

- *Your cadence.* Before, you may have had access to members of your support network weekly, or even daily. Once you enter the workforce, you need to be more intentional about when and why you reach out to people.

So how can you find the right advisers for you?

A personal adviser scorecard is a framework I created that you might find useful (see figure 20-1). It outlines the most important factors you should consider when curating your circle of advisers and is meant to improve your understanding of yourself and your needs. Doing so can provide guardrails to the sometimes ambiguous networking process and help you determine which relationships are worth pursuing and deepening.

My scorecard includes four categories, which in my experience capture the most essential attributes you should consider

FIGURE 20-1

Personal adviser scorecard

Use the scorecard below to evaluate potential advisers and build a diverse circle of people who will meet your professional and personal needs. You can update each category based on your preferences and goals.

			Does the potential adviser meet your expectations or needs?				
			Exceeds	Above/ meets most	Meets	Below/ does not meet most	Does not meet
Operating style	Support type	Tactical	○	○	○	○	○
		Emotional	○	○	○	○	○
		Sponsorship	○	○	○	○	○
		Advice	○	○	○	○	○
	Engagement methods	Face-to-face	○	○	○	○	○
		Email	○	○	○	○	○
		Phone	○	○	○	○	○
		Text	○	○	○	○	○
		Casual	○	○	○	○	○
		Formal	○	○	○	○	○
	Communication style	Encouragement	○	○	○	○	○
		Radical candor	○	○	○	○	○
		Blend	○	○	○	○	○
Expertise	Domain expertise	Marketing	○	○	○	○	○
		Sales	○	○	○	○	○
		Finance	○	○	○	○	○
		Policy	○	○	○	○	○
		Financial services	○	○	○	○	○
		Technology	○	○	○	○	○
		Consumer goods	○	○	○	○	○
	Skills type	Soft: Self-awareness, communication, emotional intelligence, curiosity, etc.	○	○	○	○	○
		Hard: Financial modeling, coding, etc.	○	○	○	○	○
	Competency	Weaknesses: (list here)	○	○	○	○	○
		Strengths: (list here)	○	○	○	○	○
Depth	Familial	Socioeconomic upbringing	○	○	○	○	○
		Familial obligations	○	○	○	○	○
		Cultural affiliations	○	○	○	○	○
		Geographic roots	○	○	○	○	○
	Personal	Faith	○	○	○	○	○
		Sexual orientation	○	○	○	○	○
		Gender identity	○	○	○	○	○
		Other	○	○	○	○	○
Extras	Personal	Charitable giving	○	○	○	○	○
		Volunteering	○	○	○	○	○
		Civic engagement	○	○	○	○	○
	Professional	Firm affinity group	○	○	○	○	○
		Nonprofit board service	○	○	○	○	○

in an adviser. Use the broad categories below as a template when developing your own unique scorecard, and expand or adjust it based on your professional or personal needs:

- *Operating style:* support type, engagement method, and communication style

- *Expertise:* industry, skills, or knowledge

- *Depth:* long-term potential and capacity for deeper conversations

- *Extras:* bonus categories based on your core values, interests, or support needs

Operating Style

Despite our instinct to group people based on jobs or backgrounds, we come in all shapes and sizes. When curating your advisers, it's important to tune into their differences and how they match up with your preferences and needs, which will likely shift over time.

Operating style is one way to think about this—it can be broken down into three categories:

Support type

This covers the kind of support you need from potential advisers, and how capable they are of giving it to you. Though support comes in many forms, to keep things simple, you can categorize it as "emotional versus tactical" and "advice versus sponsorship." Our needs usually fall somewhere on the spectrum between the two.

If you're looking to ease your fears about a job application, for example, you need emotional support. If you're looking for guidance around how to prepare for a technical job interview, you need tactical support. If you're looking to be promoted or change industries, you may need a sponsor—someone to advocate for you when you're not in the room. In all these cases, you need advice (just different kinds). When you're building out your circle of advisers, consider who would perform best in these different roles to ensure all your bases are covered.

Generally speaking, I've found that near-peers are the most willing to offer tactical support, like résumé reviews and mock interview sessions. Midcareer professionals are more qualified to offer specialized advice around their expertise, and senior leaders are best suited to serve as sponsors or provide aid on big-picture career decisions and strategy.

Engagement

This is all about format, formality, and frequency. Does your potential adviser like to chat face-to-face, over email, by phone, or through messaging apps? How soon or far out do they prefer to schedule meetings? Is this person someone you want to share regular updates with, or someone you don't mind seeing biannually?

It takes time to feel out these preferences, but you don't need to formally ask people to be your adviser to accelerate the process.

These relationships develop much like friendships. Whatever method you use, just be consistent about reaching out and maintaining the relationship. Their responsiveness is an indicator of their commitment.

Communication style

This is about what kind of feedback you find most effective, and whether the preferred communication style of your adviser candidates align with that.

Some people, for example, benefit more from words of encouragement while others prefer tough love. In my experience, it's best to have a healthy mix of people under this category. When you need a confidence boost, you'll want to connect with someone who fills you with pride; when you need to hear the unvarnished truth, you'll want someone who can deliver radical candor. In the case of sponsorship, you'll want someone who's willing to guide and be honest about what you need to accomplish in order for them to feel comfortable putting their reputation on the line and advocating for your advancement.

As you shift and grow, bring new people with styles better suited to your current situation into your circle, and negotiate the terms of your existing relationships.

Expertise

Humans are mimetic by nature. We absorb behaviors and knowledge from those we spend time with. That's why building a circle of advisers who encourage you to stretch yourself is a simple way to accelerate your personal growth and expand your mindset.

Like operating style, expertise is multidimensional and can be broken down into three categories:

Domain expertise

Domain expertise describes someone's knowledge of a specific or specialized field and typically takes two forms: functional (for example, marketing, sales, finance) or industry (for example, technology, financial services, consumer products).

If you're still figuring out what career path you want to take, you could benefit from advisers who specialize in your functional area across different industries (for example, financial services, strategic finance at a startup). If you're looking to grow within a specific industry, a circle of advisers who each specialize in different areas of that industry (or who have different functional expertise within it) may be more beneficial, as you'll have a wide variety of subject-matter experts to call on as questions or challenges arise.

In either case, taking a holistic approach to building your circle will serve you for years to come.

Skill type

Skills can be bucketed into "hard" and "soft" skills. As an early-career professional, you may be tempted to focus more on advisers who have hard skills that clearly align with your job responsibilities or interests (for example, financial modeling, coding).

But underdeveloping your soft skills (for example, self-awareness, communication, emotional intelligence, curiosity) is a risk. As you move further along in your career, and particularly if you're interested in management, you'll spend a great portion of your time using those soft skills—which recruiters are finding increasingly desirable.

As you curate your advisers, be on the lookout for people whose talents are more intangible. These softer skills can look like someone who has strong verbal and/or written communication (for example, a good storyteller, analytical writer, structured communicator whose thoughts are easy to follow). These skills could also take the form of strong interpersonal dynamics (for example, facilitating meetings in a way that brings everyone around the table into the conversation, capable of influencing others, magnetic personality).

Competency

Lastly, consider your strengths and development areas and seek out competent people in both categories. Capitalizing on your strengths will benefit you, and people who share them—especially senior colleagues—can teach you how to practice them in useful ways. Communication, for example, is one of my strengths, and being around other people who value clear communication has helped me continue to learn, develop, and take pride in that skill.

In a similar vein, you can address your weaknesses by surrounding yourself with advisers who excel in those areas. A good adviser will teach you how to improve and actively nudge you toward a higher standard. If your company has determined that certain competencies are essential to promotion, developing them is going to be essential to your growth.

Depth

"Bigger is better" is a narrative that most people are conditioned to believe, particularly early in their careers. But when it comes to your advisers, a smaller, highly curated group of people you can develop deep relationships with and who have the capacity to grow alongside you is typically better.

As you advance professionally, your career decisions will become more nuanced and include more personal factors—your partner's career, family planning, buying a home, your health, and so on. All these things can have a big impact on your choices. When you change industries, careers, or trajectories in general, your network will need to evolve with you. Choosing advisers who are invested in your long-term development will lower their churn rate.

So how do you identify these people? I'd encourage you to consider all the dimensions of your identity and add the elements that are most important to you to your scorecard. The professional world has a tendency to be reductionist when it comes to this topic, throwing people into neat boxes labeled by gender, race, or institutional affiliations. Too often, we overlook the multiplicity of what shapes us and influences how we view the world.

Consider your socioeconomic upbringing, cultural affiliations, faith, sexual orientation, geographic roots, or any other factors that impact your person, and how they fit together to make you unique. Then look for alignments in the people you meet or come across.

It can be helpful to review a potential adviser's published work, social media posts, or group memberships (on LinkedIn) to get a sense of whether your interests, dispositions, or identities align in meaningful ways. If you see things that resonate, they may be a good fit.

For example, if I were a student interested in technology and engaged with the foster care system, I might reach out to someone like Emi Nietfeld, former Google and Facebook engineer who's written about her experiences with the foster care system and homelessness, as she could speak more intimately to my experience. Similarly, if I was undocumented, interested in finance, and unsure about navigating the compliance component of hiring, someone like Julissa Arce or Charlis Cueva, who have both navigated those processes with Goldman Sachs, might be people with whom I'd able to form more intimate relationships. (Look these folks up on LinkedIn—you'll find them.)

The point is to look deeper than surface-level affinities and focus on the things that make people uniquely relatable to you. You can get personal guidance that is tailored to your needs if you make connections with this mindset early on. The more meaningful the relationship, the higher the probability it has of enduring, as emotional resonance is an essential ingredient of strong relationships.

Extras: Bonus Categories

This is a free space to fill as you wish. For example, because living a life of purpose is integral to who I am, my bonus category is purpose (for example, striving for impact beyond building generational wealth or making it the C-suite). Purpose has manifested in different ways in different periods of my life—in middle school, I tutored students at no charge in classes; in the last few years, entrepreneurship has been my chosen vehicle for service, and I have used it to build several mission-driven ventures. I see service as an integrated, lifelong practice and believe that philanthropy is a "give back" accessible at all ages and stages.

Your bonus categories should also be based on your core values, interests, or support needs. Some examples may be managing mental health, neurodivergency, caregiving, or work-life blend. Your values and needs have a strong influence on how you process career and life decisions. Having people in your network who see the world through a similar lens can be a powerful tool when making tough choices and planning ahead.

Finally, Remember . . .

Just breathe. You've been building relationships your whole life. The professional realm isn't much different from the personal. You're still making connections—you're just talking about different topics. Building a cabinet of advisers is worth doing early in your career, as influencing and stakeholder buy-in will become more integral to success as you advance. Scorecards are a good exercise to ensure you are bringing the right people close.

QUICK RECAP

You should build a circle of advisers with varying specialties who can support you throughout your career. There are four key factors to consider when curating your circle.

- **Operating style.** Observe their differences and how they match up with your preferences and needs.

- **Expertise.** They should vary in terms of background, industry, roles, or skill sets to encourage you to stretch, grow, and expand your mindset.

- **Depth.** Your group should be small—full of people you can develop deep relationships with and who have the capacity to grow alongside you.

- **Extras.** Base your bonus categories on your core values, interests, or support needs.

Adapted from "Forget Mentors—You Should Build a Circle of Advisers"
on hbr.org, June 29, 2022.

NOTES

Chapter 4

1. Abraham P. Buunk and Frederick X. Gibbons, "Social Comparison: The End of a Theory and the Emergence of a Field," *Organizational Behavior and Human Decision Processes* 102, no. 1 (February 2007): 3–21, DOI:10.1016/j.obhdp.2006.09.007.

Chapter 7

1. David M. Schweiger, William R. Sandberg, and Paula L. Rechner, "Experiential Effects of Dialectical Inquiry, Devil's Advocacy, and Consensus Approaches to Strategic Decision Making," *Academy of Management Journal* 32, no. 4 (December 1989): 745–772, https://psycnet.apa.org/record/1990-11131-001.

Chapter 8

1. Daniel J. McAllister, "Affect- and Cognition-Based Trust as Foundations for Interpersonal Cooperation in Organizations," *Academy of Management Journal* 38, no. 1 (February 1995): 24–59, https://www.jstor.org/stable/256727?seq=1.

Chapter 9

1. Dawn Heilberg, "Gen Z in the Workplace: Everything You Need to Know," *FirstUp Blog*, January 6, 2023, https://firstup.io/blog/gen-z-in-the-workplace/.

Chapter 10

1. Will.I.Am, "Yes We Can," February 2, 2008, YouTube video, https://www.youtube.com/watch?v=SsV2O4fCgjk.

2. Stephen D. Shaffer, "Balance Theory and Political Cognitions," *American Politics Quarterly* 9, no. 3 (1981): 291–320, https://doi.org/10.1177/1532673X8100900303; Yen-Sheng Chian et al., "Triadic Balance in the Brain: Seeking Brain Evidence for Heider's Structural Balance Theory," *Social Networks* 63 (October 2020): 80–90, https://www.sciencedirect.com/science/article/abs/pii/S0378873320300368.

3. Matthew Feinberg and Robb Willer, "Moral Reframing: A Technique for Effective and Persuasive Communication Across Political Divides," *Social and Personality Psychology Compass* 13, no. 12 (December 2019), https://compass.onlinelibrary.wiley.com/doi/abs/10.1111/spc3.12501.

4. Matthew Feinberg and Robb Willer, "From Gulf to Bridge: When Do Moral Arguments Facilitate Political Influence?" *Personality and Social Psychology Bulletin* 41, no. 12 (October 2015): 1665–1681, https://journals.sagepub.com/doi/10.1177/0146167215607842.

Chapter 11

1. Lee G. Bolman and Terrence E. Deal, *Reframing Organizations: Artistry, Choice, and Leadership* (San Francisco: Jossey-Bass, 2021), 303.

2. Efrat Elron and Eron Vigoda-Gadot, "Influence and Political Processes in Cyberspace: The Case of Global Virtual Teams," *International Journal of Cross Cultural Management* 6, no. 3 (2006): 295–317, https://doi.org/10.1177/1470595806070636.

3. Kathleen Kelly Reardon, *The Secret Handshake: Mastering the Politics of the Business Inner Circle* (New York: Crown Currency, rept. 2002).

Chapter 12

1. "SHRM Survey: Half of U.S. Workers Have Crushed on a Co-Worker," SHRM press release, February 11, 2021, https://shrm.org/about-shrm/press-room/press-releases/Pages/Half-of-US-Workers-Have-Crushed-on-a-Co-Worker.aspx?_ga=2.66860718.1051678378.1631091745-1735163828.1631091744.

2. Adzuna, "Two-Thirds of Brits Have Been Romantically Involved with a Colleague," HR Director News, February 11, 2020, https://www.thehrdirector.com/business-news/the-workplace/two-thirds-of-brits-have-been-romantically-involved-with-a-colleague/.

3. Sean M. Horan and Rebecca M. Chory, "When Work and Love Mix: Perceptions of Peers in Workplace Romances," *Western Journal of Communication* 73, no. 4 (2009): 349–369, DOI: 10.1080/10570310903279042.

4. Sean M. Horan and Rebecca M. Chory, "Relational Implications of Gay and Lesbian Workplace Romances: Understanding Trust, Deception, and Credibility," *Journal of Business Communication* 50, no. 2 (2013): 170–189, https://doi.org/10.1177/0021943612474993.

5. Horan and Chory, "When Work and Love Mix."

6. Renee L. Cowan and Sean M. Horan, "Love at the Office? Understanding Workplace Romance Disclosures and Reactions from the Coworker Perspective," *Western Journal of Communication* 78, no. 2 (2014): 238–253, DOI: 10.1080/10570314.2013.866688.

Chapter 19

1. Christine Comaford, "76% of People Think Mentors Are Important, but Only 37% Have One," *Forbes*, July 3, 2019, https://www.forbes.com/sites/christinecomaford/2019/07/03/new-study-76-of-people-think-mentors-are-important-but-only-37-have-one.

INDEX

ABOUT THE CONTRIBUTORS

MIMI ABOUBAKER is an entrepreneur and writer. Most recently, she founded Perfect Strangers, the largest coronavirus crisis response initiative in the United States, which delivered over 3 million meals in partnership with nonprofits and government agencies. Prior to entrepreneurial endeavors, she spent time in finance at Goldman Sachs and Morgan Stanley. For more tips on leaning in on career and life, follow her on X/Twitter @mimi_aboubaker and visit her website at www.mimiaboubaker.com.

KELSEY ALPAIO is a senior associate editor at *Harvard Business Review*.

RAINA BRANDS is an associate professor at University College London. She is an expert in social networks and how these informal workplace relationships can present hidden barriers to performance, attainment, and collaboration. A core focus of her research is to understand how social networks shape women's careers and to directly intervene in these processes to create more meritocratic organizations.

PAWAN BUDHWAR is a professor of international human resource management at Aston Business School at Aston University.

PAIGE COHEN is a senior editor at *Harvard Business Review*.

AMY GALLO is a contributing editor at *Harvard Business Review*, a cohost of the *Women at Work* podcast, and the author of two books: *Getting Along: How to Work with Anyone (Even Difficult People)* and the *HBR Guide to Dealing with Conflict*. (Harvard Business Review Press, 2022 and 2017, respectively) She writes and speaks about workplace dynamics.

ELIANA GOLDSTEIN is a certified professional career and success coach. Prior to coaching, she spent 10 years working in sales within the ad-tech industry and with various startups. As a coach, she assists her clients in learning key career strategies, building necessary mindsets, and setting goals needed to achieve the success they desire in their current roles and future careers. In light of ongoing shifts in the workplace and workforce dynamics, her focus remains on providing professional tools to develop more-engaged and fulfilled employees, thereby fostering thriving, employee-first companies.

SEAN HORAN is a professor of communications at Fairfield University.

LIANA KREAMER is an assistant professor in industrial organizational psychology at the Florida Institute of Technology. She is interested in meeting tactics and behaviors, leadership styles, and team dynamics. Find her on LinkedIn.

AILUN KU is president and CEO of the Opportunity Network. She is an alumna of New York University's Steinhardt School's Senior Leaders Fellowship and was also an MIT Media Lab Director's Fellow in 2019. She is a trained LEGO SERIOUS

PLAY facilitator and received her master of public administration from NYU's Robert F. Wagner Graduate School of Public Service and her BA from New York University's College of Arts and Science.

BEN LAKER is a professor of leadership at Henley Business School, University of Reading. Follow him on X/Twitter @drbenlaker.

ASHISH MALIK is a professor of human resources management at Queen's Business School, Queen's University of Belfast, Northern Ireland, United Kingdom.

DVIWESH MEHTA is the regional director, South Asia and the Middle East at Harvard Business Publishing.

CYDNEI MEREDITH is a first-year organizational science doctoral student at the University of North Carolina at Charlotte. She is interested in employee voice and silence, meetings, and psychological safety.

ANTOINETTE OGLETHORPE is a consultant, coach, speaker, and author with 30 years' experience developing leaders for multinational organizations. She is a Chartered Fellow of the CIPD, a member of the Association for Coaching, and a member of the Institute of Leadership and Management. Antoinette's latest book is *Confident Career Conversations: Empower Your Employees for Career Growth and Retention*.

JANICE OMADEKE is the award-winning author of *Mentorship Unlocked: The Science and Art of Setting Yourself Up for Success,* and is a global thought leader and speaker, and was the CEO and founder of the acquired mentorship software company The Mentor Method. Recognized for her distinctive viewpoints on professional development, mentorship, and inclusive entrepreneurship, Omadeke has been profiled in leading publications, including *Entrepreneur, Forbes,* and *Enterprise Magazine.*

CHARMI PATEL is an associate professor of international human resource management at Henley Business School.

JANET T. PHAN is the founder of Thriving Elements, a global nonprofit that connects underserved, underrepresented girls with STEM mentors. She is the author of *Boldly You: a Story About Discovering What You're Capable of When You Show Up for Yourself.* She is also a senior technical program manager for a company working to get affordable and reliable broadband to unserved and underserved communities globally. Her TEDx Talk is titled "3 Key Elements to a Thriving Mentorship."

NIVEN POSTMA is the managing director of Niven Postma and works as a performance coach for global executive teams, building Whole System Leadership. She's had a wide and varied career across multiple organizations and sectors in South Africa and internationally, including CEO of the Businesswomen's Association, CEO of NOAH (Nurturing Orphans of AIDS for Humanity), head of the SARB Academy at the South African Reserve Bank, and head of Leadership and Culture for the Standard Bank Group. She is a tutor at the Cambridge Institute for Sustainability Leadership, a lecturer on various global leadership development programs, and the author of *If You Don't Do Politics, Politics Will Do You.*

HOLLY RAIDER is the dean of the School of Business and a professor of management at Quinnipiac University. She mentors students, young professionals, and executives on strategy, leadership change, business transitions, and stakeholder engagement in high-stakes situations.

RAY REYES is the chief program officer of the Opportunity Network, overseeing all organizational programs and program teams. Previously, he was an assistant director and career counselor at New York University's Steinhardt School of Culture, Education, and Human Development. He received his BA in English from Rowan University and his MA in higher education from the Steinhardt School.

STEVEN G. ROGELBERG is the Chancellor's Professor at the University of North Carolina at Charlotte for distinguished national, international, and interdisciplinary contributions. He is the author of *The Surprising Science of Meetings: How You Can Lead Your Team to Peak Performance* and *Glad We Met: The Art and Science of 1:1 Meetings*. He writes and speaks about leadership, teams, meetings, and engagement. You can find him at stevenrogelberg.com.

VASUNDHARA SAWHNEY is a senior editor at *Harvard Business Review*.

RUCHI SINHA is an associate professor of organizational behaviour at the University of South Australia Business School, Adelaide, Australia. Her research explores how leadership impacts how trust, voice, conflict, and power dynamics manifest and evolve in teams to influence work relationships and performance outcomes.

NICOLE D. SMITH is the editorial audience director at *Harvard Business Review.*

ANAND TAMBOLI is an innovator, futurist, transformation expert, award-winning author, filmmaker, and keynote speaker, specializing in areas that intersect with technology and people. As an executive coach for millennials and Gen Zers, Anand often works with entrepreneurs, helping make their ideas and strategies a reality.

JEFF TAN is the director of corporate development and portfolio strategy at Agenus, an immuno-oncology focused biotech, and previously served as the chief of staff. Prior to that, Jeff helped lead strategic business insights and new product strategy at Epizyme, another small oncology biotech, and spent time working in management consulting focused on commercial strategy in the life sciences.

MELODY WILDING is an executive coach and the author of *Trust Yourself: Stop Overthinking and Channel Your Emotions for Success at Work.*

Accelerate your career with HBR's Work Smart Series.

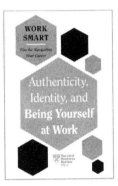

If you enjoyed this book and want more career advice from *Harvard Business Review*, turn to other books in **HBR's Work Smart Series**. Each title explores the topics that matter most to you as you start out in your career: being yourself at work, collaborating with (sometimes difficult) colleagues, maintaining your mental health, and more. **HBR's Work Smart Series** books are your go-to guides to step into and move forward successfully in your professional world.